EMOTIONAL RESILIENCE

AND THE EXPAT CHILD

PRACTICAL TIPS AND STORYTELLING TECHNIQUES THAT WILL STRENGTHEN THE GLOBAL FAMILY

FOREWORD BY DOUG OTA

First Published Great Britain 2011
by Summertime Publishing

© Copyright Julia Simens

ISBN 978-1-904881-34-6

Designed by creationbooth.com

To Jacqueline and Grant.

You have taught me every day how to launch a child towards a wonderful life. You educate me. I love you more than you will ever know.

May your lives be full of emotions and overloaded with *joy, peace, love and laughter.*

Table of Contents

Chapter 4
Ten dyads

Chapter 5
Explaining the importance
of emotions to your child

Chapter 6
Taking action - activities
for your family's stories

Chapter 7
Tying it all together - developing your family plan

Chapter 8
Dealing with hard emotions with your own children

Chapter 9
Conclusion - when in doubt connect........

Chapter 10
Closing comments ....

Acknowledgments

The writing of this book has been a wonderful experience and would not have come to fruition without the help of some exceptional people in my life.

I want to thank Jo Parfitt for guiding me through the whole process from helping me see my vision to completion of this book.

I also want to acknowledge all the educators and parents with whom I have worked over the past 20 years. I have learned so much from each one of you and have tried to share some of our experiences in this book. Thank you for loving and protecting all children and helping them grow into their unique potential. You are guardians for our children's innate emotional well-being. I always describe the feeling parents and teachers have about wanting the best for their children as 'passionate'. If we really want to build on the passionate feelings of *love* we have for our children, we need to think of how we want them to most successfully live the rest of their lives.

I want to thank my extended family and friends for all the support and 'grounding' back to the U.S.A. they have given me over the years.

Last, I want to thank Kevin Simens, who is responsible for giving our family a global perspective. Relocating and intercultural living involves many issues regarding our identity, communication, parenting decisions, and adjustments to new environments. We learned to live passionately and love our children wholeheartedly.

About the author

Julia Simens is an educator, consultant, and presenter with a focus on international relocation. This has kept Julia coming and going from the U.S.A. for over 20 years. She has worked on five continents with families who are relocating all over the world. With a focus on family therapy and early childhood education, she has helped many children and families adjust to their global lifestyle. She has worked with many embassies, multi national companies, and youth groups. She is a member of the American Psychological Association. Julia connects with children of all ages. Parents look for her for guidance because she has survived seven international moves and has raised her own two children overseas. She offers parents in cyberspace on-going support. She is a frequent speaker at educational and business conferences and has been cited in various family publications including *The Street Network, AOL Travel* and *Family Goes Strong*. Julia works in international schools where she offers children and parents individual sessions and the opportunity to grow and she conducts parent seminars as well.

Foreword

You might deserve a compliment.

But there's a problem: the person or persons who might pay you that compliment one day are simply too young to do so now.

So let me try to do so on their behalf.

The fact that you are reading—or are considering reading—this book launches you into a different category of parent. You may be about to embark on a practical journey that is likely to change your child's or children's future development in a potentially profound way. Why?

Because you might be about to equip yourself with the skills to do a better job with that most important of human tasks: the raising of children who understand themselves. The ability to understand one's self resides at the foundation of being able to truly understand anybody else—including one's own children. And this can only mean that you are about to unpack a gift that your child or children will benefit from. And their children. And so on.

I am fully aware that these are large claims. But think about it: how many hours did you go to school to earn your high school diploma? Or to earn your first college degree? Or to study to become an engineer, or an artist, or a lawyer, doctor, or diplomat?

And yet how many hours do most parents spend getting trained to become "parents"?

Around the world, in every presentation after presentation that I have given and in parenting group after parenting group that I have led, the answer is usually simple: none. Apart from the way their own parents raised them, the vast majority of parents never get any specific training for a job that is arguably as challenging—if not at times far more challenging—than engineering, law, medicine, or diplomacy. In fact, kids are expert at finding exactly those areas of their parents' "training" that were somehow left undone, generally because of issues of their own upbringing. And kids hone in on those areas like hawks. (The theory I often share in my own consulting room on why kids do this is simple: kids want "whole" parents, and they push on these unfinished areas in an existential quest to push their parents to get "completed".)

So reading any good book on parenting places the reader, in my definition at least, in the elite. Your choice of Julia Simens' book places you in a special category of that elite.

Why? Because Julia takes you to the heart of what this most important of human tasks, namely parenting, is all about: emotions. This is no "soft" or "emotional" claim. Nor is this is a "soft" book. Consider it the "basic training" that most parents skip. If a child is ever going to understand him or herself, he or she is going to have to master the signals that his or her own body transmits, signals that warn him or her that "something is up". This sounds easy, but it is not. In fact, in addition to the compliment I paid you on your child or children's behalf, let me also issue a warning: "understanding ourselves" is a skill that verges on art, and one that only a minority of the human population ever truly masters. Not understanding ourselves lies at the root of not being able to understand the other, and not being able to understand the other resides at the root of all human conflict.

This, then, is a book that can contribute to the climate in families' living rooms, as well as that between nations.

Few parenting books that I have ever encountered have ever broken the skill of understanding feelings into such easily digestible and imminently practical steps that any parent can apply. No book has ever done so with the special issues of an expatriate or mobile population in mind.

Julia's book does both, and does so beautifully.

Julia has taken her own expatriate experiences as a mother of her two children, Jacqueline and Grant, and woven them together into a story about emotions that tours the world and leaves the reader feeling whole. Her soothing, maternal voice massages the reader, page after page, bedside after bedside, linking new homes in new countries into a coherent whole that feels quintessentially centered. The reader is placed in a most privileged and intimate position: being able to listen to the bedside stories of a mother to her child. And in the repetition of those stories, month after month, in new bedroom after new bedroom, Julia shows the reader—rather than merely "telling" us—what safe human attachment sounds like. Her voice becomes her children's portable home.

And so it is perhaps only fitting that I, as a man, get an opportunity to compliment that voice and to make an appeal to the other half of Julia's potential readers, i.e. the fathers of the world. Gentlemen, this is not only a book for mothers. Every human born into this world has the same emotional "equipment", instilled through millions of years of evolution and refinement. Men, too, must find their voice in modeling for their children how they understand that equipment and their resultant feelings. This is not only a woman's work. A home, after all, has more than one entrance.

Enjoy the journey of reading Julia's book. Someday your children will thank you.

Drs. Douglas W. Ota
NIP Child Psychologist
March, 2011
The Hague, Netherlands

Introduction

Developing the emotions every child needs

The only thing you can be sure you *can* move around the world is your child's ability to thrive. In order to do this you need to help your children build up their interpersonal skills. Emotions are common in all languages and all cultures. As a parent, you can help your child build his or her emotional and basic social skills and you can do this in any location of the world. Using a wide range of emotions and the ability to understand when and why to use them are important for all children.

By the age of five children should be able to identify and relate to a wide variety of emotions. To illustrate this I have taken stories from our own travels and connected an emotion to each event that I will share with you in this book. My goal is to allow you to use this book as a tool that will help you to connect with your own child or children and to use it to build on their vocabulary of emotions.

My family

We are a family of four that hold U.S.A. passports but have not lived in the U.S.A. for most of our lives. I first went overseas as an elementary teacher then returned home for more education. I met Kevin who had also worked overseas but was back in the U.S.A. with his company. We married and started a life overseas again as soon as we could. In 1991, Jackie, our daughter, was born in Perth, Australia and three years later Grant was born. In our life of moving around it was amazing to have the same doctor for both of our children's births. This might have been the only consistent thing they have ever shared in their lives.

> There is nothing ordinary about TCKs (Third Culture Kids). They are raised on the cusp of two or more cultures: the one that they were born into and the one that physically surrounds them.

In 1999, Pollock and Van Reken stated the definition of Third Culture Kid in their book *Third Culture Kids: Growing up Among Worlds* as:

"A third-culture kid is an individual who, having spent a significant part of their develop-mental years in a culture other than their parents' home culture, develops a sense of relationship to all of the cultures, while not having full ownership in any. Elements from each culture are incorporated into the life experience, but the sense of belonging is in relationship to others of similar experience."

Like most Third Culture Kids, there is nothing ordinary about Jackie and Grant. They have had exposure to seven languages in their home (English, German, French, Spanish, Indonesian, Yoruba, and Thai). They are children raised on the cusp of two cultures, the one that they were born into and the one that physically surrounds them.

Grant, now 16, feels it is routine to fly thousands of miles and set up meetings with his friends in new or different locations. Two such meetings stand out in my mind. Several summers ago we were heading to our summer home on Roatan, Honduras, with one overnight stop over in Houston. Grant set up a movie night – not with us but with his friends from Thailand that had moved back to Texas. Another time we met up with one of his friends from the International School of Bangkok in the parking lot of an amusement park in Colorado because his friend was visiting her grandma and we were visiting our extended family at the same time.

Jackie, now 19, has a real appreciation of globalization and was quick to let me know when a recruiter from a well-known university was misinformed about the geography of Europe (luckily she corrected him under her breath). Two days later and at a different university we were subjected to incorrect political information about Asia. I did not even look at Jackie for *fear* of what her opinion might be about this blunder.

Using Robert Plutchik's major work, *Nature of Emotions* (1989), and Gordon Neufeld's *Six Stages of Attachment* (2006), I have created what I hope will be a book of stories that you can share with your children and a workbook that will help you, as parents, to connect and make lasting, valuable, family memories together.

Children who move around during their childhood need to understand themselves so they can connect to others easily and honestly. It is important that parents build a rich vocabulary around emotions so your child can distinguish between the subtle differences of joy, delight or ecstasy. Imagine how much the family can benefit when your child can let you know that he or she is bored, fed up or worn out and employs the appropriate emotion in order to do that.

Emotions are formed in the family unit

Most children spend the majority of their time at home in the family unit and so they will develop ideas about how to express emotions primarily through social interactions in their own families. Today, many children spend a significant part of their developmental years in daycare or as expatriates with additional family support in the household provided by nannies and drivers. These interactions are important. Through socialization children learn an emotional vocabulary that enables them to name internal sensations associated with objects, events, and relations that they encounter. Children learn how to express what they feel about the environment they are in and the people they are around.

This book is what many families have been looking for, particularly when they have experienced relocations. Here you will find a guide to which emotions need to be explored in order to encourage stronger, healthier, more communicative relationships. It will also raise awareness of the wide range of emotional experiences all families have as they move around the world. Find support and empathy as the stories included resonate with you.

Understanding the classification of emotions

Grab an orange and slice it in half. As you look at it, you can begin to understand how emotions can be represented in a simple way. The segments can be seen as different but still related. I like how the orange shows pairs of polar opposites. Some emotions are similar and others seem to be exact antitheses of each other. Each emotion also exists in varying degrees of intensity. When working with young children it is important for them to be able to see or understand a feeling or concept, so using an orange is a wonderful tool. You can talk about opposite emotions by pointing to one side of the orange, *joy*, and then show your child the opposite section, *sadness*.

In order to understand how to raise emotional awareness in your own child, you need to have an understanding of the theory of emotions. Robert Plutchik is a leader in classification and the theory of emotion and through this work he identifies and separates a wide range of emotions into positive and negative segments of varying intensities.

Although there are cultural differences in how emotions are expressed and then interpreted, it is clear that some emotions are universal. These are often called *basic*, *primary*, or *fundamental* emotions. These emotions form the core or foundation from which all other emotions are derived.

Primary emotions

Robert Plutchik created a wheel of primary emotions that consisted of eight basic emotions:

- Joy
- Trust
- Fear
- Surprise
- Sadness
- Disgust
- Anger
- Anticipation

The eight basic emotion dimensions could be described by words such as *ecstasy*, *admiration, terror, amazement, grief, loathing, rage* and *vigilance* or other synonymous terms reflecting differences in intensity. Plutchik (1962) believes these basic emotions are primary and all other emotions derive from them.

Emotional dyads

This workbook will also cover what are known as *dyads*. A dyad is a mixture of primary emotions. Robert Plutchik first developed the idea of the dyad with follow-up work by T.D. Kempler and Jonathan Turnerr (1987). We know that emotions are not literally mixed like primary colors. Emotions are a lot more complex in our brains and bodies; however, this analogy helps us understand how basic and complex emotions are generated.

Looking at the primary dyads of the adjacent emotions, *joy* and *acceptance*, they lead to *love*. For example – you are expecting your second child so everyone is getting very excited. There is a lot of time talking about the 'new arrival'. Your oldest child experiences *joy* when she sees her younger brother. Yet, it is only after she has *acceptance* for her brother does she *love* him.

We will be looking at these emotional dyads. They are:

- Optimism
- Submission
- Awe
- Disapproval
- Remorse
- Contempt
- Aggressiveness
- Love

We will also look at two emotions that young children need to understand:

- Grief
- Serenity

Throughout this workbook, I will include a dictionary term (*OED*) for each emotion we are sharing. There will also be a child-friendly version to help with your child who is under five-years-old. In order to help with understanding the concepts in this book, at times I refer to your child in gender-neutral terms. I use 'he' to refer to your child.

How children reach their potential

I believe that experiences in the early years of your child's life deeply impact him for the rest of his life. Having a close connection to a parent allows him to reach his potential.

Talking about emotions helps young children understand their feelings. The key factor for understanding emotions in these young children is predicted by their overall language ability. Your child has to be able to explain why he feels the way he feels and be able to communicate that to others. One factor that may contribute to the social difficulties of children with limited language ability is emotional competence. Research by Fujiki, Spackman, Brinton and Illig (2008) found that children with language impairment do not recognize emotions as well as children their own age with typical language development.

Language

I always encourage parents to speak in the language that is most familiar to their child when it comes to talking about emotions. This rich language base of the parent can help define and explain the differences to their child. Many expatriate children have multiple home languages. When you factor in the host country language or languages of staff members in the household it can be confusing for a young child to understand emotions.

Children may have difficulty when the language of the school is not their first language. In International schools, where English is the medium of instruction, many parents stop speaking to their children in their first language or mother tongue. Parents think they should speak English all the time. It is important to maintain the mother tongue to ensure cognitive growth.

When you move your children around the world they face cognitive and emotional challenges as their learning involves both a new language and a new culture with each move. Children, especially those who spend time with second language learners, will need support to clearly understand emotions. Children need to have the ability to identify and label feelings. The reason why some children are good at this and others are not comes down to the child's family model or approach in talking about emotions.

> The strongest deterrent to teenage high risk behavior is a strong emotional connection between your child and yourself. Good relationships create resilience to dangerous acting out behavior in your child.

Research shows that early childhood connections to parents are vital. Summarizing the results of a two-year study of 12000 teenagers, gender researcher Dooley (1999) wrote, "researchers discovered that the best predictor of a teenager's health and the strongest deterrent to high-risk behavior was a close relationship with a parent. They concluded that a strong emotional connection with at least one parent or significant adult figure reduces the odds that an adolescent will suffer from emotional stress, have suicidal thoughts or behavior, engage in violence, or use substances (tobacco, alcohol, or marijuana). Good relationships help create resilience to dangerous, acting out behavior in your children." As parents, you owe it to your children to create that close connection. This book will help to show you how.

The importance of attachment

In order to forge that vital close connection, you need to understand the way healthy relationships develop. Psychologist Gordon Neufeld presents six stages of attachment that create the foundation for virtually every relationship your child will ever have, beginning with parents, and later with siblings, friends and intimate partners. This attachment is the cornerstone of parenting. It can help with keeping your child on track academically, managing challenging behavior, and maintaining the all-important role of being the one they turn to for advice and support.

There are many possible scenarios that outline a typical family group. Some children form an attachment to a carer other than a biological parent. Many children with a single working parent, or in families with nannies or other key people who do child rearing, form their attachments to these key people. Same families have an absent parent or a 'late' parent, for example, an adopted child at age five. Some families have a main income earner that is often gone or some families have a parent that travels a lot; these children learn to attach to key members and form special bonds to their parents when they are around.

The six stages of attachment

Interestingly, children move through the stages of attachment at a rate of about one stage per year.

1. The most primitive and basic stage of attachment is Proximity. Through touch, contact, and closeness, the infant begins attaching to his or her parents.

2. Secondly, toddlers seek Sameness with their parents, mimicking their mannerisms or dress, and looking for ways to be the same as their parents.

3. The third stage is Belonging or Loyalty. Often three-year-olds will be very possessive and say "my mommy or my daddy".

4. Four-year-olds seek reassurance of the strength of their attachment to parents by wanting evidence of their Significance. This is the fourth stage.

5. The fifth stage develops around the age of five when we see the beginnings of genuine Love as attachment goes deeper and deeper.

6. And finally, the sixth stage. From age six onward, if the attachment roots have gone deeply enough, we have a child who allows him or herself to venture out into Being Known.

In his work, Dr. Neufeld explains that all relationships will follow these six stages:

- Proximity
- Sameness
- Belonging/Loyalty
- Significance
- Love
- Being Known

Each stage solidifies the attachment between parent and child. If any of the areas are weak then the relationship itself will weaken.

Naming emotions

Children that have 'emotional literacy' are able to identify and understand emotions as well as respond to emotions in themselves and others in a healthy manner. If your child has a strong foundation in emotional literacy he or she can tolerate frustration better, get into fewer fights, and engage in less self-destructive behavior than children who do not have such a strong foundation.

> The ability to name a feeling will allow your child to discuss and reflect with you about his or her personal experience of the world.

The ability to name a feeling will allow your child to discuss and reflect with you about his or her personal experience of the world. The larger your child's emotional vocabulary, the finer discriminations he or she can make between each of their separate feelings and the better they can communicate with others about these feelings. Children who are able to label their emotions are on their way to becoming emotionally competent. In the following two scenarios, you can see a larger variation in the children's ability to label the feelings of frustration.

Let me begin to illustrate this in action with a story:

WE HAVE REACHED OUR CRUISING ALTITUDE NOW

I am on an international flight between Perth, Australia and Reno, Nevada, U.S.A. I am traveling with six-month-old Grant and three-year-old Jackie. I started the flight already sleep-deprived

and worried. Several hours into the flight a child sitting in the row in front of us has a problem.

A four-year-old boy is an avid paper thrower. As he searches the seat pockets in vain for yet another piece of paper to throw, his initial calm hunt becomes more hurried and disorganized. When he begins to yell and disrupt many more rows of seats, the parents try to intervene. He finally aggressively approaches his older sister who looks frightened.

"Doug, what's the matter?" his mother leans in and asks.

Doug screams that his sister, Ann, has his paper and proceeds to reach across to get it. His mom stops him for grabbing the paper, whereupon Doug launches into a major tantrum. This continues for way too long. Way. Too. Long.

Jackie is three-years-old. She loves to play with small plastic dolls and animals, making towns, zoos, and stores and so on in which they can all interact together. She has made a wonderful block area on her airline seat table. About thirty minutes into her play, she crosses her arms across her chest and frowns.

"Jackie, what is the matter?" I ask, leaning across.

"I want to make it bigger."

"Hmmm . . . that's not possible, your table is full," I reply beginning to sense her frustration.

"I'm mad!" she pouts.

"Are you really mad or upset . . . or frustrated?"

"Yeah, I'm frustrated and a little mad."

"You feel frustrated and a little mad, well that's a problem. What can you do?"

Jackie thinks and thinks, looks around the small crowded airline rows and frowns again.

"I can let you have the zoo part of the town and when I get the stores done, we can switch them around," she decides.

I go back to reading my book.

Doug was unable to communicate how he was feeling. Because of his lack of emotional knowledge he was unable to express to his mother his feelings and hence, this led to behavioral problems. Jackie, a year younger, had the ability to voice her feelings. This ability led to her social competence on a crowded airline flight that resulted in a more enjoyable time for everyone. The ability to label emotions is a developmental skill that is not present at birth – it must be learned.

> The ability to label emotions is a developmental skill that is not present at birth - it must be learned.

Parents need to act as guardians for their children's emotional and social growth. If we want to channel the passionate feelings of *love* we have for our children into a healthy approach to raising them, we need to think about how we want to prepare them to most successfully live the rest of their lives.

Benefits of reading our emotion stories

The young child will gain awareness of the conventions of reading (left to right, top to bottom). Your child will gain vocabulary. Running your index finger under the print as you read will let your child notice that printed words have meaning. Most children under the age of six like to hear the structure of a story and the sameness of the passages. Repetition makes it easier for your child to pick up on the patterns in the sounds you make. Sometimes it is best to choose a place free from distractions so you and your child can give undivided attention to the story. This is why bedtime reading is ideal for many families. Read slowly and with expression. Children *love* to hear their parents use sound effects. Pause while you read, and ask your child what he or she thinks will happen next. Seek out his or her reactions to events in the short story.

Children who are ready for the reading process will like you to point to the words as you read them. This helps your child develop one-to-one correspondence for words. With all ages, check for comprehension of the story periodically by asking questions about what you have read.

If your child is unable to explain the emotion in the story, you can use the terms as I have outlined them to help your child understand what the emotion means. With older children encourage them to practice reading out loud. You can offer to read every other page or you can read the emotion and geography portion of the story and let your child read the short story.

Talk with your child. Talking makes your child think more about his experiences and helps him expand his vocabularies. Ask your child to give detailed descriptions of events and to tell complete stories.

Share your stories

Share your stories from around the world, talk about the emotions involved in the stories and then create your own memories of emotions that your family has experienced. After you complete this workbook you can send your favorite stories to me at *julia.simens@gmail.com*. I will be sharing the emotional stories that you have created with your child on my blog at http://www.jsimens.com.

Join me in this global journey with your children around the world and prepare yourself to make memories starting today.

Julia Simens
M.A. Clinical Psychology Child,
Adolescent, and Family Therapy
Counseling Coordinator
Bangkok, Thailand
March 2011

> To children who successfully navigate a lifetime of change, the world is a garden of exotic gifts, a house of treasure to explore and take in. Transferred from place to place, young and porous, global nomad children collect and absorb experiences. Their personalities become amalgams of those cultures they internalize and claim as their own. Perched for a while in a new environment, they experience each move as an occasion for growth, a chance to blossom in new ways.."
> – Unrooted Childhoods – Memories of Growing Up Global

Plutchik's Three-Dimensional Model of Emotions

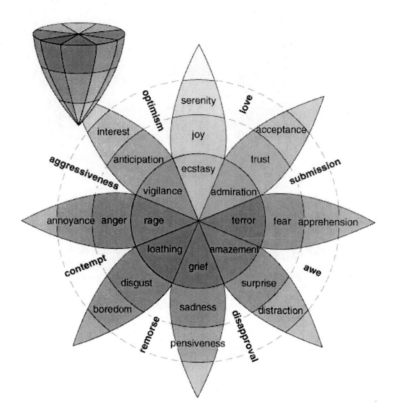

All 'emotion photos' in Emotional Resilience and the Expat Child were taken by their peers when they were exploring a unit of Inquiry on "How we express ourselves".

Chapter One

Working with emotions and understanding them

Throughout this workbook you will find that I include a dictionary definition of the emotion about which you are reading. This will ensure that both you and your child are absolutely clear about the meaning of that emotion and share the same understanding of it.

Some people are able to hide their emotions, while others are like an open book. Although no one teaches us the meaning of emotional expression *on* the face, most of us believe we can read emotions from people's faces. Parents will attest to the fact that they are the experts when it comes to reading their own children's faces!

> "Thought is deeper than all speech;
> feeling deeper than all thought." – Christopher Cranch

Most people believe they know what emotions are. They think of emotions as special kinds of feeling that they label with such words as *happy, sad, angry,* or *mad.* We all recognize that emotions are a part of our daily lives and they are constantly being expressed in direct or subtle ways in our relationships to children, parents, friends, co-workers, and lovers. We assume the listener understands these terms because of similar experiences and through their resulting empathy with us. What should you do, though, if the listener does not know what a word such as *anticipation* or *disgust* means? It is up to you, as a parent, to help build your child's emotional vocabulary through their experiences.

The *Oxford English Dictionary (OED)* is the most extensive summary in existence of the origins and meanings of English words. Sometimes it is helpful to examine the origins, the etymology, of am emotion word. Let's look at *anger* and its synonyms of *annoyance, fury,* and *rage.*

The word *anger* come from a Norse word that means *trouble* or *afflicted*. It can mean physical affection or pain. *Annoyance* comes from a French word related to the modern word *ennui*. The *OED* defines this term as a "mental state akin to pain or to affect a person in a way that causes a slight irritation". The word *fury* comes from a Latin word which means to be mad. The word *rage* comes from the Latin word that means rabies or a disease that may occur as the result of the bite of an animal. It may also mean a violent act or a furious passion.

This suggests that the language of emotions is complex and derives from different historical sources, and is used inconsistently. It is no *surprise* that scholars have difficulty deciding on a single, unequivocal meaning of an emotion term in any language. This is why it is so important for you and your child to work on your emotion stories together so you build up a common understanding of these emotions.

Identifying the language of emotions

Take a sheet of paper and see how many emotions you can list. For many this is a quick and easy task, but after coming up with a long list of 30 to 40 words they find it gets much harder. Now compare your list with someone else's in your family. You will likely find that there is inconsistency among everyone in decoding which words are emotion words and which are not.

> We use different words to convey emotions. We may also interpret differently the emotional degree of these words.

Generally people use different words to convey emotions but also they may interpret differently the emotional degree of these words. This is why many research groups collect and classify huge numbers of words that might be emotional words. Storm and Storm (1987) in *A Taxonomic Study of the Vocabulary of Emotions*, asked several hundred children and adults to list every emotion word they could think of. They were also asked to label the feelings of characters in clips from commercial televisions shows. Together, the children and the researchers were able to come up with a list of over 200 terms, which is pretty impressive, and certainly more than even an adult would normally come up with alone. Children, understandably, have a hard time doing this alone too. They need a loving caring adult to support their emotional growth and to direct them towards the emotional skills they need to be successful.

Inconsistency for young children is due to several reasons:

1. Parents often use the words in different grammatical forms, such as adjectives (*angry*), nouns (*joy*) and verbs (*saddened*). This creates some confusion for a child.

2. Parents use words that are strange or uncommon to their child, such as *discombobulated, antsy* or *badger*. Sometimes children are just unfamiliar with some words.

3. Sometimes parents present words that are out of context. This adds to the ambiguity of the terms and confuses the young child. Sometimes parents will shorten their thoughts and speak in 'baby

talk' and it can cause a young child to be confused. Imagine the effect on a three-year-old who is busy playing if his mother shouts from across the room "ice cream" meaning "let's go get ice cream" but the child hears "I scream" meaning "I am so mad that I am going to scream."

So many emotions

There are a small number of basic emotions. All other emotions are secondary, derived mixtures or blends of the primary ones. Theorists all agree that there are a few basic emotions that qualify as *primary emotions*. The smallest number is three and the largest is 11, while most studies list five to nine emotions. This section covers some of the most noted philosophers' or psychologists' lists of basic emotions.

- Hindu philosophers stated eight basic or natural emotions (Schweder and Hoidt, 2002):

  - Sexual passion, love or delight
  - Amusement, laughter and humor
  - Sorrow
  - Anger
  - Fear or terror
  - Perseverance
  - Disgust
  - Amazement

- Rene Descartes, French philosopher (1596-1650), said there were only six primary emotions. He called them passions:

  - Love
  - Hatred
  - Desire
  - Joy
  - Sadness
  - Admiration

- Baruch Spinoza, a Dutch philosopher (1632-1677), mainly saw emotions as caused by cognitions. He felt there were only three primary affects:

  - Joy
  - Sorrow
  - Desire

- Thomas Hobbes, British philosopher (1588-1679), felt there were seven simple passions:

  - Appetite
  - Desire
  - Love
  - Aversion
  - Hate
  - Joy
  - Grief

- Silvan Tomkins (1911-1991) is best known as the developer of Affect Theory and Script Theory. He assumed there were nine basic emotions:

  - Interest/Excitement
  - Surprise/Startle
  - Enjoyment/Joy
  - Dissmell (reaction to bad smell)
  - Distress/Anguish
  - Fear/Terror
  - Shame/Humiliation
  - Disgust
  - Anger/Rage

- Robert Plutchik's (1927-2006) research interests included the study of emotions, the study of suicide and violence, and the study of the psychotherapy process. He considered eight primary emotions:

  - Fear
  - Anger
  - Sadness
  - Joy
  - Acceptance
  - Disgust
  - Anticipation
  - Surprise

"I suppose leadership at one time meant muscles; but today it means getting along with people."   - Mohandas Gandhi

Understanding emotional intelligence (EQ)

For many people the work on Emotional Intelligence, known as EQ (rather than Intelligence Quotient (IQ)) by Daniel Goleman is their first introduction to the importance of building emotional intelligence. Daniel Goleman (1995) makes the case for 'emotional intelligence' being the strongest indicator of human success. He defines emotional intelligence in these terms:

- Self-awareness
- Altruism
- Personal motivation
- Empathy
- The ability to love

The ability to love is defined as being loved by friends, partners, and family members. Goleman feels people who possess high emotional intelligence are the people who truly succeed in work as well as play, building flourishing careers and lasting, meaningful relationships.

> The ability to love is defined as being loved by friends, partners, and family members. People who truly succeed in work as well as play, building flourishing careers and lasting, meaningful relationships, have high emotional intelligence.

Goleman's book, *Emotional Intelligence*, is based on brain and behavioral research. In his work he looks at pilot programs in schools from New York City to Oakland, California, where kids are taught conflict resolution, impulse control, and social skills. He proposes these basic families of emotions:

- Fear (Safety), anxiety, apprehension, nervousness, concern, consternation, misgiving, wariness, qualm, edginess, dread, fright, terror, and in the extreme cases phobia and panic.

- Anger (Justice), fury, outrage, resentment, wrath, exasperation, indignation, vexation, acrimony, animosity, annoyance, irritability, hostility, and perhaps these are manifest in the extreme as hatred and violence.

- Sadness (Loss), grief, sorrow, cheerlessness, gloom, melancholy, self-pity, loneliness, dejection, despair, and depression in the extreme case.

- Enjoyment (Gain), happiness, joy, relief, contentment, bliss, delight, amusement, pride, sensual pleasure, thrill, rapture, gratification, satisfaction, euphoria, whimsy, ecstasy, and at the far edge, mania.

- Love (Attraction), acceptance, friendliness, trust, kindness, affinity, devotion, adoration, and infatuation.

- Disgust (Repulsion), contempt, disdain, scorn, abhorrence, aversion, distaste, and revulsion.

- Surprise (Attention), shock, astonishment, amazement, and wonder.

- Shame (Self-control), guilt, embarrassment, chagrin, remorse, humiliation, regret, mortification, and contrition.

Because emotional intelligence isn't fixed at birth, Goleman feels adults as well as parents of young children can sow the seeds.

A dictionary label for emotions

Given the various labels described above, is it possible to prepare a definitive list of emotions in the English (or any other) language? For many parents it is hard to break down such common thoughts or feelings. I believe that the number of possible emotions is limitless because each family has a social situation, labels the emotions in that situation, and then socializes their child to recognize them.

Oxford English Dictionary

e·mo·tion

1. An effective state of consciousness in which *joy, sorrow, fear, hate,* or the like, is experienced, as distinguished from cognitive and volitional states of consciousness.

2. Any of the feelings of *joy, sorrow, fear, hate, love,* and so on.

3. Any strong agitation of the feelings actuated by experiencing *love, hate, fear,* and so on and usually accompanied by certain physiological changes, as increased heartbeat or respiration, and often overt manifestation, as crying or shaking.

For a young child, emotion means, "How are you feeling, what is your body feeling like?"

The most important thing to remember when trying to get your child to 'learn' something new is to take clues from them on how much they are ready to listen or how much they are asking to learn.

> ## General Principles for Working with Emotions
>
> 1. Recognizing emotions is the basis of self-knowledge and interaction.
>
> 2. Emotions are connected with your own memories and observations, bringing them to mind when needed.
>
> 3. Working with emotions may be more exhausting than mental or physical struggle.

ROUGH LANDING

My eighteen-year-old daughter, Jackie, attended one month of her total elementary and high school life in an American school – the month before we moved to Indonesia. We had just moved back to the U.S.A. after spending five years in Australia. We had no idea that as soon as we bought our house, major appliances, lawn mower, dog, and two cars that we would be heading back overseas to a new job. The movers had an easy job – they just added new red number stickers over the yellow stickers since some of our boxes had not been unpacked. Somehow between the chaos of repatriation and the uprooting to a new assignment we added one month of kindergarten for our first-born.

The young sport-dressed teacher is excited that the classroom has someone from out of the area.

"Good morning class!" calls out Miss Black.

"Good morning!" the class sings back.

"I am very happy to introduce Jackie to you all. Jackie is a new student from out of state. Can you say good morning to Jackie?"

"Good morning Jackie!" Fourteen smiling little five-year-olds chant back.

Jackie is wearing her favorite blue jeans and a brightly colored top. Her face displays a beautiful smile. Initially Jackie is eager to get into the classroom but with all the attention directed at her, she slides her small hand on my pants leg and looks up at me. I do not feel it is my place to correct her new teacher that Australia is not a state but a country.

"Have a really special day, Jackie," I quickly say as I bend down to kiss her cheek before ducking out of the room.

Later that night as we are going over what happened today and how Jackie feels about kindergarten, she starts to cry.

"What is upsetting you?" I ask, pulling the covers up around her neck.

"I am not from outer space," Jackie whimpers.

I just stare at her trying to make some sort of logical connection to the tears and this statement. As I sit down on her bed she explains her whole day at school and the stress her teacher has caused for her with the opening comments about Jackie being new to the school.

I am at a loss for words but know that Jackie needs my support to understand her first day in kindergarten.

Try to explain to your five-year-old the difference between an Australian accent and an American accent. Then explain that "out of state" is not "outer space". Then explain that her teacher misspoke, while trying to not put the teacher in the wrong light. Without laughing, try to ascertain whether any of her classmates felt she was from 'outer space'. It was a long conversation. Here is part of it:

"Jackie, how did you feel when your teacher said 'out of state – or outer space'?"

"I knew she was wrong but I was surprised she didn't know Australia was in this world."

"What else did you feel?"

"I was really really scared that the kids would believe her!"

"Were you really – really – scared, or just a little afraid?"

"Not too scared, but afraid."

"Afraid but maybe even a little bit nervous about the new school?" I suggest.

"Nervous, yes maybe," Jackie reaches for her favorite toy, Little Turtle, and hugs him tightly.

"Were you really afraid?"

"No, I was nervous . . . but still surprised she didn't know about Australia," Jackie replies, determined to get the last word in before bedtime.

Jackie needed time to process her feelings, but she also needed help in seeing that her feelings of being *scared* also could exist in various degrees of intensity. Spending time and helping her distinguish the levels between *scared, a little afraid* and *nervous* helped Jackie's emotional vocabulary grow.

Children who successfully handle transitions still need to have support and understanding from their parents that transition takes effort to be successful, even if you are used to moving.

Families that move need to make sure that recurring things such as going to a new class or moving to a new school are not lightly passed over or treated like 'no big deal'. Even children who successfully handle transitions like this need to have the support and understanding from their parents that transition takes effort to be successful, even if you are used to moving. Knowing we would be encountering lots of new school situations in our travels around the world, it was important for me to have Jackie understand the difference between being *scared*, a *little afraid,* or *nervous.*

Research shows that moves tend to disrupt younger children's education, particularly when they are developing the basic skills of reading, writing, and math. Dr. Elmore Rigamer, a child psychiatrist, found that while older children have more difficulty adjusting *socially* following a move, younger children have more difficulty adjusting *academically.* The move itself interrupts the continuity in development of basic skills. Once those skills are in place, moves become easier and students can keep up with their schoolwork more easily, even following a transition. I believe the foundation for an even easier transition is expanding the emotional intelligence of your children. If they have a firm foundation in understanding and applying their feelings to actions and reactions they will be able to understand themselves and others better.

> "Children . . . often are the forgotten piece in . . . relocation packages."
> – Vicki Poulson-Larson,
> writing on corporate programs, in Mobility magazine

Strategies for expatriate families

Expatriate families leave their support system of grandparents, siblings, extended families, primary care physicians, and close friends to experience life in other parts of the world. Not having these consistent connections makes it hard for the whole family. There are no guarantees that one strategy or another will make the difference for young child during these moves, but there are two strategies that we know have helped children:

1. Open lines of communication

Every family will have its own process for dealing with change, but repeated studies and anecdotal evidence indicates that if a family works together to keep open lines of communication and, while acknowledging their own frustrations and challenges during this period, parents manage to stay generally upbeat, usually children will do the same.

2. Family comes before work

Every child must know that he/she is more important to his or her parents than the employment that first took the family to the new location. Just saying this is not enough. This concern and care for the children that overrides work considerations must be shown through attitudes and actions. If children know this intuitively, most are then able to accept the change and eventually carve out a space for themselves in the new environment. Spending time with your child to create these emotion-memories will help deliver this message to your children.

Parenting is Hard Work

When our children perceive us as steady and calm regardless of their moods or behavior – they can relax, knowing they can rely on us to get them through the challenging moments of their lives.

What have you learned?

Complete the following learning table

Think

What thoughts or reflections do you have about this section?

Talk

What three things would you like to talk about and discuss with others?

Apply

What will you apply and turn into a habit?

Chapter Two

Attaching to parents (and carers)

Many cultures raise their children in extended village families, where the babies are always 'attached' to someone, giving them security. This is not as common in the expatriate population where caregivers can be interchangeable due to moves. Although the attachment relationship is universal, our parenting beliefs and practices do differ around the world. Attachment practices are those responses that caregivers use to develop a deep and lasting connection with their child. There is an increasing number and diversity of these practices with all the movement of people around the world.

Attachment influences early brain development, which has an impact on a child's lifelong abilities to regulate thinking, feelings and behavior. Families bring with them a wealth of experience, knowledge, and skills regarding child-rearing practices that in many cases have been traditionally passed down from generation to generation. Children may display different attachment behaviors according to what is considered culturally appropriate within a particular community. Although there is a strong intuitive component to attachment relationships, children learn to behave in a way that gets them what they need. I urge parents to *trust* their own judgment and 'listen' to their child, even if their decisions are contrary to those of friends or family.

> ### Proximity – First Stage to a Strong Connection
>
> When you invite a child to be in your company, you're promoting proximity. This most basic invitation to be near your child – whether it is a cuddle, playing a game, or working on this book together – sends a message to your child that you want to be close and connected.

The bond of an adult to a child

Since I feel so intensely about the bonds of an adult to a child, I decided that making a workbook for you to experience together with your child would create the perfect connection. There is only one ideal way to work closely with young children – you have to get physically close to them. They need to see your eyes so you need to be down at their level. They need to hear you without you being too loud or demanding so you need to lean in towards them and speak gently. You need to be close enough that your child can smell you and feel your presence. This is a 'comfort' for many young children. It can also mean *love* for a teenager even if at times they appear to not want you close.

Hazan and Diamond (2000), in *The Place of Attachment in Human Mating,* pointed out the similarities between infant caregivers' attachment and adult romantic love. Close proximity and contact define attachment behaviors in children. Both types of love usually have a preoccupation with touching, caressing and kissing. Children wish to share discoveries and reactions with their attachment figures, and lovers typically like to share gifts with each other. Childhood attachments can lead to baby talk and a special quality of mothering talk. Adult lovers also sometimes use baby talk and a special type of playfulness. Hazan and Diamond conclude that this approach to understanding love offers a developmental perspective on this complex emotion. Many parents have never analyzed what makes a good relationship with their child, it just happens. If you have the understanding of what works in relationships then it is easy to see when you are getting off target.

> Proximity sends the message you want to be close and connected. This is important to all children, especially teens when they appear to not want you around.

Concept of opposites

When I start to work with children on building an emotional vocabulary, I like to begin with the concept of opposites. Children love to talk about opposites and many children's picture books cover topics such as, short/tall, big/small, and hot/cold. I usually start my consultations with the emotions *happy/sad*, but to build up your child's vocabulary we will use the word *joy*.

BASIC EMOTION	OPPOSITE EMOTION
Joy (Happy)	Sadness (Sad)
Acceptance (Like)	Disgust (Not Like)
Fear (Scared)	Anger (Mad)
Surprise	Anticipation

It is hard to work with any emotion in isolation. Your child will usually pair up emotions because he likes to understand extremes. There is no right or wrong way to use this book. Some parents go directly to the emotion that they feel their child needs to work on; other parents will go smoothly from one emotion to the next. If emotions seem to be hard for your child to express or understand then you need to start at the emotion that is the easiest for them to connect with. I encourage you to do what feels right for your family.

Families adapt and change

With seven international moves under our belt my family feels confident that we have had some unique experiences and yet some common ones too, that many families may have encountered. As a family, we have had to learn how to adapt to different countries, schools, curriculums, climates, cultures, and religions. We learn to laugh and cry as we try to understand the current culture in which we live. Emotions are worldwide. Humans interpret and use a repertoire of about one hundred emotions in their routine interactions.

> Humans interpret and use a repertoire of about 100 emotions in their routine interactions.

Steven Gordon (1990), in *Social Structural Effects on Emotions,* asserts that the origin of emotions is not in biology but in culture. Children who straddle several cultures as they move around the world, and children who live daily in multicultural homes, need to have the firm foundation of understanding emotions.

Emotion language and culture

Inevitably, research on children's use of emotion words depends on those children being old enough to use words. As a result, most research is done on children from two or three-years-old to adolescence. Sometimes researchers ask the parents to provide recollections of emotional words. Sometimes parents are asked to keep a diary to record the use of emotional words as well as the contexts. Some researchers show children pictures of emotions or films of interactions between children then ask them how the various children in the film feel.

These studies show that by the age of two to two-and-a-half children have the ability to make some 'correct' inferences about emotions in pictures. By two-and-a-half, 50 per cent of the children interviewed can identify *happy* faces and some can identify sad and mad faces. By four-years-old, *happy* is understood by almost all children. Generally by five, they know surprised and scared. By seven-years-old, almost all know *sad* pictures. But if children are presented with short descriptions of events that might cause them to feel a particular emotion, four-year-olds can usually identify *happiness, sadness, anger, disgust,* and *surprise* (Camras and Allison, 1985). When facial expressions are videos of actors creating each expression for five seconds, most four-year-olds can discriminate *happy, sad, mad, surprised,* and *scared.*

There are a number of reasons why the study of emotions is difficult. Among them is the fact that the language of emotions is complex and often ambiguous. People are aware that they, and probably others, disguise or hide their feelings for various social reasons. We often do what our culture informs us is normal or expected. The expectation of air travel is often that children belong in the back of the plane. If they are allowed in the business section, they should remain quiet and others should not notice them.

DEBBIE!

I am flying on a long international flight with my three-year-old and my five-year-old. We have a large travel bag full of fun and wonderful things to keep us all occupied. We had a 3:40 a.m. check in at Jakarta so that started the day in a new and interesting way. The six-hour flight to Tokyo was uneventful, the two-hour layover was nice to stretch out our legs, and even the nine hours on into the U.S.A. was palatable for all three of us. We have made it across the Pacific Ocean and everything is going great. We hit the U.S.A. airport customs area and the stress level starts to rise for us all. As usual, I am a single flight parent. Either the work schedule for my husband is too demanding or he is just very bright! In order for me to get the most out of the travel experience, I often leave home sooner in order to let the children spend more time with their grandparents and extended family.

As the customs officials ask us the general questions, I find I can't even respond to "Where are you coming from?" I mutter something about "Tokyo" as Jackie voices "Jakarta" and Grant says "Tarta!" in his loudest big boy voice. Somehow we make it into the U.S.A. When we get on the short flight from Seattle to Denver, I know we can survive the two and a half more hours of travel. I am dead tired. After we take off, I see both children are sound asleep so I nod off. I can only imagine what happened while I was asleep.

"Do you want any crackers?" Jackie asks Grant.

"Yes."

"I get to tickle you before you get a cracker!"

"Okay."

Grant loves to eat goldfish crackers so I am sure the tickle marathon started with each goldfish cracker creating more and more excitement. As excitement grows, I am still asleep.

"Jackie, stop tickling me now," says Grant, tired of the game.

Jackie continues to tickle without even giving any goldfish crackers.

"Jackie, stop it."

"I can't, you didn't say it right."

"Stop it."

"No, in American you have to say Deb-bie," Jackie is quick to say with authority. *"Deb-bie means stop it."*

I believe the event continues on with a tickle session given by Jackie, a loud "Deb-bie" stated by Grant and on and on. And on. And on. With each "Deb-bie" getting louder and louder. I start to wake up and move around. Both children appear to be angels as I come back to conscious awareness of the airplane and people around me. We buckle up and make a perfect landing.

As we exit the plane a rather strange conversation is held.

"Thanks for flying with us today," a smartly dressed flight attendant smiles to us. She leans down to eye level with Jackie and says, "You must be Debbie."*

"No, I am Jackie," she smiles, proud to be noticed.

"Where is Debbie?" asks the attendant.

"I don't know," replies Jackie.

"Who are you, big boy?"

"I'm Grant," says Grant again in his loudest big boy voice.

"Excuse me, Madam, do you want to wait for your other child?" asks the attendant.

I have no idea what she is talking about. "No, two is enough for me." I replied as we left the airplane.

Later that evening as I hear Jackie and Grant playing in Grandma's living room, I hear a strange exchange. Grant is saying "Deb-bie" and he is saying it often. As I go in to investigate, I hear the story about how Jackie was sure using Deb-bie was the correct American term to mean stop it. I knew and she knew she was just pulling one over on Grant and yet he was eager and ready to accept her older and wiser knowledge on how to fit into the American society. Even at the age of three Grant was aware that he might not know how to fit into a society that he is a part of but does not live in.

I wonder how long the flight attendant worried about that third child. Or how loud my children were actually on the flight. Or how a goldfish cracker ended up in my bra. All expats understand the unspoken culture of airline travel. Even though the flight may be made up of many different cultures there are some societal expectations. Often your child will be expected to not make noise, to not play ,and to not even touch the seatback in front of them. With understanding, love, and compassion, your child learns to adapt to all of these different social situations.

> "Life is a train of moods like a string of beads"
> – Ralph Waldo Emerson

Facial expressions and reactions

Your child may not understand that his face and inside feelings are clues to his emotions. Some children need help to understand how their face and body language are good indicators of what they are feeling.

To help your child connect his feelings with his body clues, try this game:

The How Did You Feel game

Ask your child to think of different times when he felt *happy, sad, afraid,* or *angry.* Then pretend he is in those situations. Have him try to describe how he feels on the inside and how his face feels. Feelings of happiness usually mean smiles, laughter, and lightness. Frowns, crying, and heavy feelings are for *sadness. Fear* is connected to tension, wanting to hide, and a tight feeling in the face. *Anger* can make them feel like they're going to explode and can cause a snarling look on their face. There are three key things to remember:

1. **Understanding complex feelings** – Emotions such as *guilt* and *shame* may be very confusing to children. They may blame themselves for a divorce or the death of a parent. Explain to the children exactly what is happening in their family, and this can help them deal with these emotions.

2. **Showing your own emotions** – Another way to help children understand and deal with their emotions is to let them see how adults cope with theirs. When adults *feel sad, ashamed, guilty,* or *happy*, they can talk about how they feel. This lets the child know that it's okay to have these feelings too.

3. **Thinking about feelings** – Emotions are not automatic. Different people will feel differently about things. Our emotions are also formed by what we think about different situations. When your child is feeling badly about something, encourage him to try to look at it in a different way.

By helping your child explore his own thinking, he may realize that his thoughts aren't clear or don't make sense. By understanding more clearly, your child may realize that blaming himself or being ashamed doesn't make sense.

Four universal emotions

I have often worked in international schools where it is common to have over 50 different nationalities on campus. There are major differences in cultures, but emotions have a likeness or resemblance in most adults and children.

The authorities on emotions all agree about the universal emotions.

They are:
*   Happiness
*   Fear
*   Anger
*   Sadness

Izard, *The Face of Emotion* (1971) began conducting research on the development of emotion knowledge years ago in Paris, and discovered that the ability to detect signals in facial expressions depicting the basic emotions crosses cultural boundaries. He conducted his research by showing a set of photographs to people from different cultures. He generally got the same answers regardless of where the people were from. Izard found that children's ability to match emotions' expression and the names of emotions grew from about age two to 10-years-old.

Seven universal facial expressions

There are major differences in cultures but happiness, fear, anger, and sadness are universal emotions. They have a likeness or resemblance in most adults and children.

If you are unsure of where to start in the process of creating these memories, the work by Paul Ekman, *Facial Expression and Emotion* (1993) might be beneficial. He has dedicated his career to researching emotions. He determined that there are seven facial expressions that are found worldwide regardless of cultural differences or emotional differences in the population. They are:

- Fear
- Sadness
- Anger
- Joy
- Surprise
- Disgust
- Contempt

These seven facial expressions are characteristic of basic emotions and are seen throughout the world.

> "Having lived on four continents, each continent looks completely different, but there are a couple of similarities that aren't seen by the naked eye. You can feel these similarities: they are love, madness, enthusiasm, sorrow and sympathy."
> – Grant Simens (age 10) Spirit of Saint Valentines

Bodily expressions of emotions

We all know that other parts of the body than the face are used to express emotions. Apart from facial expressions you have: the erection of body hairs; the flushing of your skin; the raising of your shoulders; and restless pacing. All reveal something about your emotional state. People often say one thing but imply another by their tone of voice or by a gesture. The range of nonverbal communicative behaviors is large. In fact studies prove that around 70 per cent of our communication comes from body language, about 20 per cent from the tone we use, and that just seven per cent of our communication is derived from the words we use. This causes even more confusion for young children. Many children are exposed to this type of nonverbal communication: facial expressions, eye movements, gaze direction, gestures, posture, voice qualities such as pitch and inflection, speech hesitations, non language sounds such as laughing, yawning, or grunting, use of social space, and touching. No wonder your children can become confused or even stop trying to understand what is being communicated to them.

The following chart describes the relationships among emotion concepts. It is helpful to understand how the emotions connect and form overlapping feelings. Take a few minutes and think how you show each of these emotions in your own face and body expressions.

Breakdown of Advanced Emotions

ADVANCED EMOTION	COMPOSED OF	ADVANCED OPPOSITE EMOTION
Optimism	Anticipation + Joy	Disappointment
Love	Joy + Trust	Remorse
Submission	Trust + Fear	Contempt
Awe	Fear + Surprise	Aggressiveness
	Surprise + Sadness	Optimism
Remorse	Sadness + Disgust	Love
Contempt	Disgust + Anger	Submission
Aggressiveness	Anger + Anticipation	Awe

> To have a rich life we need to laugh and be connected. To have a balanced life, we have to have highs and lows. We need to give children a variety of experiences.

Most people feel that to have a 'rich' life they need to have experiences that make them laugh and feel connected. In reality, to have a balanced life, you need to have highs and lows. You have to give your child a variety of experiences. He needs to know what it is like to sit quietly and read a good book. He needs to know what it feels like to run wild in rain puddles. He needs to know how to nurture and care about other people. With your new or expanded understanding of emotions, you are ready to help your child expand his emotional understanding. In this workbook, I have given you a foundation of emotions that your child should know and be able to express. Therefore I included the 17 fundamental emotions for you and your child to explore that is in the above chart. The 18th emotion I included is *grief.*

What have you learned?

Complete the following learning table

Think

What three thoughts or reflections did your child have about this story?

Talk

What emotions in these stories are the easiest for your child to express?

Apply

What could you apply for your own family's emotional growth?

Chapter Three

Eight primary emotion stories

This chapter contains short stories that take place in a variety of locations. The emotions are described in these short stories. Then it covers why the location is so unique. Some of these stories were from Jackie's experiences around the world and some were from Grant's. In order to make it more predictable for young children to read or understand, I have made each story be about a boy called Jack. How you choose to read this book to your child depends on your child's age.

If you are reading to a two or three-year-old, sit with them in your lap or lie down next to each other. Let them hear your voice acting out Jack's words and his mother's words with two different voices. Let him see the pattern in the stories.

If you are reading to a four or five-year-old, you can ask them if they know what is coming next. You can take turns being Jack and repeat his words after they are read. You can also do as suggested above.

If you are reading with an older child, ask him what he would like to do. How would he like the story to be read? Would he like you to read the dictionary and location page and he could read the story page?

See if your child can take some of their own experiences and place them into our emotion stories. Most children can relate to other children. Ask your child, "When did you feel like Jack?"

The locations of the primary emotion stories

The expatriate lifestyle usually allows families to live or travel to unique locations. Talking to your child about his experiences will help expand his emotional vocabulary.

Our initial eight stories take place around the world. I will be taking you to Australia, the Cook Islands, and Egypt, where you will experience *joy, surprise,* and *anticipation.* Then you are off to South Africa, Thailand, and Indonesia to experience *fear, anger* and *disgust.* Since many of our emotion stories revolve around the stories of children in international schools, please note that international schools can be in any location in the world. You will experience *sadness* at one international school. The expatriate lifestyle usually allows families to go to live in unique locations and it builds on geographical skills due to the ability to travel on relocation and during vacation time.

Joy

Oxford English Dictionary

1. A vivid emotion of pleasure arising from a sense of well-being or satisfaction; the feeling or state of being highly *pleased* or *delighted*; *exultation of spirit*; *gladness, delight*.

2. The expression of *glad feeling*; outward *rejoicing*; *mirth*; *jubilant festivity*.

3. A source or object of *joy*; that which causes *joy*, or in which *delight* is taken; a *delight*.

For a young child: Your face is really, really *happy*. You feel wonderful. You might even want to dance. This is *joy*.

Geography

You can experience *joy* while swimming with the dolphins at Monkey Mia. Monkey Mia is a remote spot geographically; it lies on a long, thin peninsula within Shark Bay in Western Australia. The water is warm and absolutely beautiful. As you stand in knee-deep water, wild dolphins come right up to the white shell beach and swim around you. Wild dolphins have been coming to Monkey Mia for over 50 years. It is the only place where dolphins visit daily, not seasonally, and it is free. It is a World Heritage landmark. If you are lucky you might get to swim with a mother dolphin and her calf.

Joy

The evening ritual begins. The sun starts to set and Jack rubs his eyes. As Jack and his mom start the short walk across the beach to their beachfront villa, she asks him, "What was your day like?"

"Let me think about it," Jack grabs her hand, looks up with a smile and continues the walk.

"How was your day?" she leans over and asks again as he snuggles into his bed.

"Mommy, I had a good day today. What should I dream about tonight?"

"Dream about what you experienced today," she softly says as she leans closer and smoothes his pillow.

"Mommy, I am thinking about all the *joy* I saw today. I am going to dream about that baby dolphin and how he stayed so close to his mother. I am going to remember the smiles on everyone's faces as the mommy dolphin swam right up so close to you. I will remember their *joy* when they realized that the dolphin picked you to swim with because both of you were having a baby. I am going to remember my *joy* when I saw you with the mommy dolphin and how you laughed and played with her. I am going to remember how much *joy* I had when I got to touch a baby dolphin. Mommy, that is what I am going to dream about."

"Do you know how much I *love* you?"

"You *love* me a lot."

"More than you will ever know," she says as she smiles and kisses him good night.

He just smiles and snuggles down in bed pulling the covers up towards his chin.

"Mommy, I *love* mommy and baby dolphins. Good night, Mom."

"Good night, Jack."

Surprise

Oxford English Dictionary

1. The (or an) act of assailing or attacking unexpectedly or without warning, or of taking by this means; sudden attack or capture of a fort, a body of troops, etc. that is unprepared.

2. The (or an) act of coming upon one unexpectedly, or of taking unawares; a sudden attack.

3. Something that takes one by *surprise*; an unexpected occurrence or event; anything unexpected or astonishing.

For a young child: You didn't know! It made you laugh. Your body feels excited. You are surprised.

Geography

You can experience *surprise* when a Picasso fish nibbles your finger at Aitutaki. Aitutaki is one of the fifteen islands in the heart of the South Pacific that make up the Cook Islands. It is a magnificent and remote island that consists of three volcanoes and twelve coral islets. Not only is Aitutaki an interesting place, the fish are interesting. The Picasso triggerfish have one of the longest names in the world. They are called Hu-mu-hu-mu nu-ku nu-ku-a pu-a-a. This is a Hawaiian name that means 'fish with a pig-nosed face'. These fish enjoy the shallower waters inside the reef where there are lots of rocks and crevices to hide in and search for food. They can be very aggressive.

To travel to Aitutaki, you have to fly from New Zealand to Rarotanga and then take a small plane or boat to this unique island. Its nearest neighbors are Tahiti to the east and American Samoa to the west.

Surprise

Time goes on. The evening ritual continues.

The sun starts to set across the lagoon; Jack rubs his eyes. As Jack and his mom start the short walk across the hall to his hotel room, she asks him, "What was your day like?"

"Let me think about it," Jack grabs her hand, looks up with a smile and continues the walk.

"How was your day?" she leans over and asks again as he snuggles into his bed.

"Mommy, I had a good day today. What should I dream about tonight?"

"Dream about what you experienced today," she softly says as she leans closer and smoothes his pillow.

"Mommy, I am thinking about how I was so *surprised* today. I am going to dream about fish and how you never know what they might do next. I was so *surprised* that a Picasso fish would swim up to me and grab my candy on the stick. But I was more **surprised** that he bit my finger while trying to get the candy. Who would have ever thought a fish would eat sugar candy on a stick! Or that I was fish bait! Mommy, that is what I am going to dream about."

"Do you know how much I *love* you?"

"You *love* me a lot."

"More than you will ever know," she says as she smiles and kisses him good night.

He just smiles and snuggles down in bed pulling the covers up towards his chin.

"Mommy, I *love* all types of surprises. Good night, Mom."

"Good night, Jack."

Anticipation

Oxford English Dictionary

1. Operating in advance, intuitive preconception, prior knowledge, intuition, precognition, and presentiment.

2. Apprehending beforehand, looking forward, expectant.

3. Prior action that meets beforehand, provides for, or precludes the action of another.

For a young child: You can't wait, it is like the morning of your birthday! You think it is going to be great; you are smiling and can't wait.

Geography

You can experience *anticipation* when you are in eastern Egypt. The Valley of the Kings is located on the west bank of the Nile River at Luxor and is one of the most important archaeological sites in the world. Seeing the Tombs of the Pharaohs is an event worth waiting for. It is a World Heritage site where you can view the royal tombs. The valley holds about 60 burial sites. Some of the tombs have graffiti written on them from ancient tourists.

Many people know about the Valley of the Kings, but there is also the Valley of the Queens where wives and children of Pharaohs were buried. In ancient times, it was known as Ta-Set-Neferu. This means the place for the Children of the Pharaoh. Seeing history in its original setting is wonderful.

Anticipation

Time goes on. The evening ritual continues.

The sun starts to set across the skyline and the pyramids are seen in the distance. Jack begins to rub his eyes. As Jack and his mom start the long walk down the hallway to his bedroom, she asks him, "What was your day like?"

"Let me think about it," Jack grabs her hand, looks up with a smile and continues the walk.

"How was your day?" she leans over and asks again as he snuggles into his bed.

"Mommy, I had a good day today. What should I dream about tonight?"

"Dream about what you experienced today," she softly says as she leans closer and smoothes his pillow.

"Mommy, I am thinking about *anticipation* today. I like that feeling, waiting for my birthday or waiting for Christmas morning! I am going to dream about how I waited and waited to finally get to see the Egyptian pyramids and the Valley of the Kings. I studied about hieroglyphs and the ancient tombs so I was so eager to get to see them in person. I couldn't wait to walk the same desert sands that ancient pharaohs walked. Mommy, that is what I am going to dream about."

"Do you know how much I *love* you?"

"You *love* me a lot."

"More than you will ever know," she says as she smiles and kisses him good night.

He just smiles and snuggles down in bed pulling the covers up towards his chin.

"Mommy, I really liked the fact that the ancient civilization liked mommies and children enough to give them Ta-Set-Neferu. Good night, Mom."

"Good night, Jack."

Fear

Oxford English Dictionary

1. A sudden and terrible event; peril.

2. The emotion of pain or uneasiness caused by the sense of impending danger, or by the prospect of some possible evil.

3. A state of alarm or dread.

For a young child: You are very *scared*. Your tummy is all knotted up and your head is pounding. You might want to run away but you are too *scared* to move.

Geography

You can experience *fear* when you are with the lions on a safari in Africa. Port Elizabeth is a city in South Africa situated in the Eastern Cape Province east of Cape Town. You can choose to sleep in cabins overnight or in the lions' hunting area in a tent with a park ranger guarding you. Near the Addo Elephant National Park is a private game viewing reserve. They have over 2000 animals and if you are lucky you might be able to see the 40 different mammal species including the free roaming lions.

In a natural habitat, Africa's Big Five, the African elephant, black rhinoceros, Cape buffaloes, lions, and leopards, all roam around together. The members of the big five were chosen for the difficulty in hunting them and not their size. You can see safari animals from the aardwolf to the wildebeest. You can watch groups of gazelle, bushbuck, eland, kanu, and kudu animals move across the plains. The aardvarks and warthogs are equally fun to watch.

Fear

Time goes on. The evening ritual continues.

The sun starts to set and Jack rubs his eyes. He looks out the window and sees Cape Town's skyline and the magnificent flat-topped Table Mountain. As Jack and his mom start the long walk home through the most beautiful city in the world, she asks him, "What was your day like?"

"Let me think about it," Jack grabs her hand, looks up with a smile and continues the walk.

"How was your day?" she leans over and asks again as he snuggles into his bed.

"Mommy, I had a good day today. What should I dream about tonight?"

"Dream about what you experienced today," she softly says as she leans closer and smoothes his pillow.

"Mommy, I am thinking about how I was so *afraid* last night. I am going to dream about sleeping with the lions in South Africa and what *fear* feels like. I know we were safe in the safari hut and that the park ranger was going to stay up all night to make sure the lions did not come into our camp, but when we heard the lions roar I was *afraid*. I was *afraid* for the wildebeest and the antelopes. I was afraid for the gazelles and even for the warthogs. It was so quiet but that was when the lion was stalking its prey. This was when I was the most *afraid*. Mommy, that is what I am going to dream about."

"Are you sure you want to dream about *fear*?"

"Hum, I think I will dream about how I overcame my *fear* and how great it really was to sleep with the lions."

"Do you know how much I *love* you?"

"You *love* me a lot."

"More than you will ever know," she says as she smiles and kisses him good night.

He just smiles and snuggles down in bed pulling the covers up towards his chin.

"Mommy, I feel safe tonight. Good night, Mom."

"Good night, Jack."

Anger

Oxford English Dictionary

1. That which pains or afflicts, or the passive feeling, which it produces; trouble, affliction, vexation, sorrow.

2. The active feeling provoked against the agent; passion, rage, wrath, ire, hot displeasure.

For a young child: You are really, really mad. Your hands are clenched in a fist. You are frowning and it feels like you want to hit something.

Geography

You can experience *anger* when you are at the Sanctuary and Rescue Center for Elephants in Northern Thailand located in the Chiang Mai Province. This center was set up to provide sanctuary for distressed elephants from all over Thailand. What makes you angry is the horrendous conditions the elephants had to endure before they were saved. The emphasis is on rescue and conservation rather than entertainment shows or training so your *anger* goes away as you watch the elephants recover in a natural environment.

Elephants are officially classified as an endangered species. There are between 3000 to 4000 elephants in Thailand. Elephants form their own social groups and they even have different personalities. The Sanctuary and Rescue Center is always adding to their herd, as they look for elephants in desperate need of care.

> "Fear and anger boiled up in my head like liquid air."
> ¬ – Ross MacDonald

Anger

Time goes on. The evening ritual continues.

The sun starts to set and Jack rubs his eyes. As Jack and his mom start the pleasant walk along the Chao Phraya River in Bangkok, she asks him, "What was your day like?"

"Let me think about it." Jack grabs her hand, looks up with a smile and continues the walk.

"How was your day?" she leans over and asks again as he snuggles into his bed.

"Mommy, I had a good day today. What should I dream about tonight?"

"Dream about what you experienced today," she softly says as she leans closer and smoothes his pillow.

"Mommy, I want to dream about our trip to Chiang Mai last week."

"What happened there that you want to dream about?"

"Mommy, I am thinking about how I was so *angry*. I am going to dream about the elephants I saw in the Elephant Sanctuary. I got to meet over 30 rescued elephants and each one had a unique approach to life at the park. It seemed like each elephant had a personal story to tell. I liked that the sanctuary increases awareness about the plight of the elephants. It also educates people on the humane treatment of their elephants. But I am still *angry* that people would hurt an elephant just to get them to do tricks for a tourist to raise money.

Mom, that is what I am going to dream about."

"Do you know how much I *love* you?"

"You *love* me a lot."

"More than you will ever know," she says as she smiles and kisses him good night.

He just smiles and snuggles down in bed pulling the covers up towards his chin.

"Mom, I love elephants and I love the people that help them even more. Good night, Mom."

"Good night, Jack."

Disgust

Oxford English Dictionary

1. Strong distaste or disrelish for food in general, or for any particular kind of dish or food; sickening physical disinclination to partake of food, drink, medicine, etc.; nausea, loathing.

2. Strong repugnance, aversion or repulsion excited by that which is loathsome or offensive, as a foul smell, disagreeable person or action, disappointment, ambition, etc.; profound instinctive dislike or dissatisfaction.

3. To excite physical nausea and loathing in (a person); to offend the taste or smell of.

For a young child: Your nose is all squished up, you want to say 'yuck' and shake your head back and forth, no, no, no. It is yucky.

Geography

You can experience *disgust* when you see the young children in the slums of Jakarta living on the East Cipinang trash dump slum. Most of the poverty-stricken children are born to poor parents. What *disgusts* you is the government policies and discrimination that allow these children to live in such horrendous conditions. Jakarta is the capital and largest city of Indonesia. It is located on the northwest coast of Java. Part of the biggest problem is getting clean water.

Children in the dump are engaged in some kind of economic activity. They can be called trash pickers and they search through the trash to find anything that might be used again or sold. Most kids contribute their earnings to their family. Some kids even attend school on the dump.

Expat children are lucky; they can easily get involved in community service and make a real impact or difference in a local family's life. Your child is never too young to start this type of 'learning'.

Disgust

Time goes on. The evening ritual continues.

The sun starts to set and Jack rubs his eyes. As Jack and his mom start the short walk down the hall to his bedroom, she asks him, "What was your day like?"

"Let me think about it." Jack grabs her hand, looks up with a smile and continues the walk.

"How was your day?" she leans over and asks again as he snuggles into his bed.

"Mommy, I had a good day today. What should I dream about tonight?"

"Dream about what you experienced today," she softly says as she leans closer and smoothes his pillow.

"Mommy, I am thinking about how I was so *disgusted* today. I hated the dumpsite where families were living. I don't want to dream about the junkyards in Jakarta and wonder why kids have to live like that. Why can't they go to school? Why can't they have clean water? Why do they have to work when they are so young? I want to dream about a better life for these children. Mommy, that is what I am going to dream about."

"That's a good dream, Jack. Do you know how much I *love* you?"

"You *love* me a lot."

"More than you will ever know," she says as she smiles and kisses him good night.

He just smiles and snuggles down in bed pulling the covers up towards his chin.

"Mom, do you know how lucky I am? I am very lucky. Good night, Mom."

"Good night, Jack."

Trust

Oxford English Dictionary

1. Confidence in or reliance on some quality or attribute of a person or thing, or the truth of a statement.

2. Confident expectation of something; hope.

3. To have faith or confidence; to place reliance; to confide. To have faith or confidence in; to rely or depend upon.

For a young child: You feel good, you know what is going to happen. You stay calm.

Geography

You can experience *trust* when you are only three-years-old and you can obey the rules on Turtle Island. As we travel in the North Andaman Sea to the tiny mountainous island of Koh Ra, which can only be reached by a long tail boat, the captain keeps telling us that a three-year-old would never leave the baby turtles alone. As we walk across the bamboo bungalow that is tucked away under a canopy of trees I explain to the children the importance of watching the turtles and not touching them. This underdeveloped beach is one of the last nesting sites for leatherback turtles in Thailand.

The island is a secluded nature resort with diving and eco-tour activities. Reef Check Thailand carries out coral reef and marine monitoring programs. They collect data from reef surveys that describe the health and condition of key ecological features in the spectacular Andaman Sea.

Trust

Time goes on. The evening ritual continues.

The sun starts to set and Jack rubs his eyes. As Jack and his mom start the short walk up to the bedroom, she asks him, "What was your day like?"

"Let me think about it," Jack grabs her hand, looks up with a smile and continues the walk.

"How was your day?" she leans over and asks again as he snuggles into his bed.

"Mommy, I had a good day today. What should I dream about tonight?"

"Dream about what you experienced today," she softly says as she leans closer and smoothes his pillow.

"Mommy, I am thinking about how the boat captain had to *trust* us today. I am going to dream about all the tiny, tiny turtles and the huge enormous turtles. I am going to dream about how you can find these 'global' turtles all over the world. They have been as far north as Norway and Alaska. They even go into the Arctic Circle. Then you can find them as far south as the Cape of Good Hope in Africa and the southernmost tip of New Zealand. Mommy, that is what I am going to dream about."

"Do you know how much I *love* you?"

"You *love* me a lot."

"More than you will ever know," she says as she smiles and kisses him good night.

He just smiles and snuggles down in bed pulling the covers up towards his chin.

"Mom, these turtles are a little like me, they travel all over the world. Good night, Mom."

"Good night, Jack."

Sadness

Oxford English Dictionary

1. The condition or quality of being *sad* (in various senses).

2. Gravity of mind or demeanor; seriousness, soberness, staidness.

3. Gloomy appearance; dark or somber hue.

For young children: Your face is almost crying. You want to hang your head. You keep your eyes down towards your feet. You sigh really loudly while you take a deep breath.

Geography

You can experience *sadness* when your friends leave your international school. *Sadness* is an emotion characterized by feelings of *disadvantage*, *loss* and *helplessness*. Third Culture Kids (TCKs) often have unresolved *grief* due to the amount of loss they experience as they move around the world.

Often children may be thinking, "I was just getting to know my friends, oh great — more goodbyes and I was just starting to feel good." The frequent breaking-off of relationships due to relocations may often cause *sadness* in children.

Sadness

Time goes on. The evening ritual continues.

The sun starts to set and Jack rubs his eyes. As Jack and his mom start the short walk up the stairs to his bedroom, she asks him, "What was your day like?"

"Let me think about it," Jack grabs her hand, looks up with a smile and continues the walk.

"How was your day?" she leans over and asks again as he snuggles into his bed. He is no longer smiling.

"Mom, I had a very *sad* day today. My friends are leaving my school. I'm sad. What should I dream about tonight?"

"Dream about what you experienced today," she softly says as she leans closer and smoothes his pillow.

"Mom, I am thinking about how *sad* I was today. I am going to dream about my entire list of friends who will be leaving this year from my school. Did you know someone from my cross-country team is leaving? My best friend who arrived here the same time I did is also leaving, and two kids that I always go to the movies with will be going. Mom, that is what I am going to dream about tonight. What will I do without my friends?"

"I know you will miss your friends. How are you feeling?"

"*Sad, very sad.*"

"Do you want to dream about being sad?"

"Yes, because I will miss my friends, but I also want to dream about new friends. Well, maybe I won't dream of being *sad*. I am already looking forward to new people arriving at my school. Since I am on student council, I will be involved in the new student orientation. Maybe I will get a new friend when I help all the new students settle into our school."

"Do you know how much I *love* you?"

"You *love* me a lot."

"More than you will ever know. Maybe you can keep in touch with your friends. Perhaps you will get to know some of the new kids coming to your school." She smiles and kisses him good night.

He does not smile but just shrugs his shoulders and snuggles down in bed pulling the covers up towards his chin.

"Good night, Mom."

"Good night, Jack."

Later on, when they had all said, "Good-bye" and "Thank you" to Christopher Robin, Pooh and Piglet walked home thoughtfully together in the golden evening, and for a long time they were silent.

"When you wake up in the morning, Pooh," said Piglet at last, "what's the first thing you say to yourself?"

"What's for breakfast?" said Pooh. "What do you say, Piglet?"

"I say, I wonder what's going to happen exciting today?" said Piglet.

Pooh nodded thoughtfully.

"It's the same thing," he said.

– A.A. Milne,
The complete Tales and Poems of Winnie-the-Pooh

What have you learned?

Complete the following learning table

Think

What three thoughts or reflections did your child have about this story?

1.

2.

3.

Talk

What emotions in these stories are the easiest for your child to express?

Apply

What could you apply for your own family's emotional growth?

Chapter Four

Ten dyads

One of the most important messages that you can give your children is that their feelings are real and okay. It is easy to let children talk about their feelings when they're *happy* and *proud*. When they're feeling *angry* or *sad*, however, it's easier to pretend that they don't feel this way. Let them talk about their feelings and help them understand them and when you do, you'll be helping your child figure out what's going on and how to deal with difficult emotions. Dyads are often harder for your children to understand.

> Feelings are social. Joy, sadness, anger, elation, jealousy, envy, despair, anguish, and grief - all these feelings are partly social. They are influenced by cultural ideas and images, and refracted through roles and relationships.

When talking about the sociology of emotions there is some key research that should be noted: the anthropologists George Foster (1972) on *envy*, Robert Levy (1973) on the *depressive emotions*, the sociologists Kingsley Davis (1936) on *jealousy*, and William Goode (1964) on *love*, F. Gross and G. Stone (1964) on *embarrassment*, the psychoanalyst Geoffery Gorer (1964) on *grief*, and the philosopher Sartre (1948) on the *nature of emotion* – all these helped clear the way for a sociology of emotions.

The premise they all suggest is this: feelings are social. *Joy, sadness, anger, elation, jealousy, envy, despair, anguish,* and *grief* – all these feelings are partly social. They are influenced by cultural ideas and images, and refracted through roles and relationships.

Belonging or Loyalty – the Third Stage to a Strong Connection

This stage strengthens attachment by emphasizing to your child that you are unequivocally his champion on his side. When you stand up for your child, you're reinforcing his need to know that he can lean on you. One of the most painful experiences is when a child does not feel his parents are his allies, such as when his parents takes the side of the teacher when there's a problem at school. Or when a parent does not have an opinion on the behavior of other children as they interact towards their child. Parents need to be their child's 'cheerleader'.

In sociology, the word 'dyad' is a noun used to describe the smallest possible social group, in other words, of two people. When you examine a long list of emotion terms usually two or three of the basic primary emotions are *components*. Sometimes a single word can represent a *mixture*. Sometimes a group of words better describe the mixture. This means they all share a common meaning and they tend to be synonyms. For example, the dyad of *disgust* and *anger* creates *contempt*. *Contempt* can also mean *hatred* or *hostility*. If your child is feeling *contempt* he could have *rage* if his anger is really strong. It is important for your child to see how these words connect and to see that they are similar. It is also important for him to understand that they vary in different degrees of strength.

Common language of emotions

The problem of establishing names for emotion mixtures is not easily solved. It is somewhat like the problem of naming colors. The National Bureau of Standards published a *Dictionary of Color Names* and gave guidelines on designating colors. It was created so people working in a number of fields could speak a common language. If emotions had a similar understanding around the world it would be easier for your child to comprehend.

"Ever since the language of man began to develop, words or expressions have been used first to indicate and then to describe colors. Some of these have persisted throughout the centuries and are those which refer to the simple colors or ranges such as red or yellow. As the language developed, more and more color names were invented to describe the colors used by art and industry and in later years in the rapidly expanding field of sales promotion. Some of these refer to the pigment of dye used, or a geographical location of its source. Later, when it became clear that most colors are bought by or for women, many color names indicative of the beauties and wiles of the fair sex were introduced, such as French Nude, Heart's Desire, Intimate Mood … The dictionary will serve not only as a record of the meaning of the 7,500 individual color names listed but it will also enable anyone to translate from one color vocabulary to another."

– Kelly and Judd, 1955 p. 5 1955 National Bureau of Standards Dictionary of Color Names

Questions to ask your child about feelings

I encourage parents to ask these questions and take notes of what their child says about these feelings. If you ask your child to write their comments they might be more involved in correct spelling and handwriting, they will not focus on the actual emotions we are trying to get them to acknowledge. So please just scribe what they talk about when you ask these questions. First, remind them there is no right or wrong way to answer these questions. They can think about the question and answer it later. Do not force them if they are not ready.

- Some kids like you say that they feel all mixed up inside. Do you ever feel like that?

- What do you try to do when you have confusing feelings?

- Boys and girls have lots of different feelings about their families. When you think about our family, how do you feel?

- When was there a time that you felt *optimism*? What were you doing?

- How do you look when you're *happy*?

- How do you feel on the inside when you are *happy*?

- Think of a time when you were *sad*. What made you *sad*?

- How do you look and feel when you're *sad*?

- How do you feel when you are *grieving*?

- Have you ever felt *ashamed* or *guilty*?

- Can you tell me about when people feel *ashamed* or *guilty*?
- What made you feel like that?

- How you feel sometimes depends on how you think about things. Can you think of a time when you felt bad and then thought about something that made you feel better?

- What was that like?

Dyad stories and their locations

Our ten dyad stories take place around the world. I will be taking you to Nigeria, the United States of America, and Indonesia. We will be exploring *acceptance, grief,* and *optimism.* Then we are off to Cambodia, Switzerland, and Honduras, where we will discover *awe, aggressiveness,* and *apprehension.* We will then experience *disapproval, serenity,* and *love.* Many of our emotion stories revolve around the stories of places we call **home**. The expatriate lifestyle is one that causes families to call a variety of locations 'home'.

> " [. . .] one of the major areas in working with TCKs is that of dealing with the issue of unresolved *grief. They are* always leaving or being left. Relationships are short-lived.
>
> At the end of each school year, a certain number of the student body leaves, not just for the summer, but also for good. It has to be up to the parent to provide a framework of support and careful understanding as the child learns to deal with this repetitive grief. Most TCKs go through more grief experiences by the time they are twenty than monocultural individuals do in a lifetime."
>
> – David Pollock, Trans World Radio, 1987

Acceptance (submission)

Oxford English Dictionary

1. To take or receive a thing offered willingly, or with consenting mind; to receive a thing or person with favor or approval, e.g. to receive as a prospective husband. Also, to take or receive with patience or resignation, to tolerate.

2. The act or fact of accepting, or taking what is offered, whether as a pleasure, a satisfaction of claim, or a duty.

3. The condition of being *submissive, yielding,* or *deferential.*

For a young child: It seems okay. It doesn't make you *happy* or *sad,* it is just the way it is. You shrug your shoulders up and down.

Geography

You can experience *acceptance* when you live in Nigeria and people dying from malaria become just a fact of life. You know many people who have survived malaria but you also know that some children and adults die from malaria. Malaria is a mosquito-borne disease caused by a parasite. In the World Malaria Report, 2008, an estimated 247 million cases of malaria led to almost 881,000 deaths, with over seven per cent of those deaths among African children under five years of age.

Statistics from UNICEF, DESA, UNDP, and WHO change each year, but those related to malaria never cease to amaze the world. One way to help combat malaria is the use of long-lasting insecticidal nets for children to sleep under. Many expatriate children are actively involved in fund raising for these nets.

Acceptance (submission)

The evening ritual begins. The sun starts to set and Jack rubs his eyes. As Jack and his mom start the short walk up the stairs to his bedroom, she asks him, "What was your day like?"

"Let me think about it," Jack grabs her hand, looks up with a smile and continues the walk.

"How was your day?" she leans over and asks again as he snuggles into his bed.

"Mommy, I had an *upsetting* day, today. What should I dream about tonight?"

"What was so *upsetting*?"

"Our driver's daughter has malaria and he is very *worried* about her."

"Did he take her to the clinic?"

"Yes, and he has her on medicine. I think she will be okay."

"I'm glad he took her to the doctor. Dream about what you experienced today," she softly says as she leans closer and smoothes his pillow.

"Mommy, I am thinking about how some places in the world are just too hard on kids. I am going to dream about *acceptance* and how malaria is a fact of life in Nigeria. I am going to dream about how malaria is both preventable and curable but over one million people die of malaria every year. The ones that are the most risk at are the babies and young children. Most of them are from Africa. Mommy, that is what I am going to dream about. We have to accept this fact but dream about changing it."

"Do you know how much I *love* you?"

"You *love* me a lot."

"Let's hope more and more people dream about changing this. I *love* you more than you will ever know," she says as she smiles and kisses him good night.

He just smiles and snuggles down in bed pulling the covers up towards his chin and pulling the mosquito netting around his bed.

"Good night, Mom. I *love* doing what we do to help the kids in Lagos. I *love* 'Feed the Needy' projects and helping support bed netting projects. I *love* living in Africa."

"So do I. Good night, Jack."

Grief

Oxford English Dictionary

1. Hardship, suffering; a kind, or cause, of hardship or suffering.

2. *Grievous, grave; troublesome, oppressive; formidable.*

3. Mental pain, *distress*, or *sorrow*.

4. Deep or violent *sorrow*, caused by loss or trouble; a keen or bitter feeling or *regret* for something lost, *remorse* for something done, or *sorrow* for mishap to oneself or others.

For a young child: You are so *sad* that you cry until your tummy hurts. Your heart feels very very *sad*, and it is almost broken.

Geography

You can experience *grief* when a grandparent dies in the United States, when you recall all the fun summer times you had with your grandma and you know you will miss her on the shores of Lake Tahoe, Nevada. Incline Village is a small town in the Sierra Nevada Mountains located at 6,229 feet above sea level on a lake that is 22 miles long and 12 miles wide.

The water is often turquoise with brilliant blues. The water is cold due to the melting snow that fills the lake. The large boulders are fun to swim around and the sand is soft and warm. Building sand castles in this environment is a perfect childhood pastime.

Expat families can experience the death of a loved one when they are not in the same location when one passes over. Besides the normal *grief* associated with loss, your family might also feel some *remorse* in regard to your own views on the situation. Often expatriates feel *guilty* that they not been able to spend as much time with their immediate family members. It is important to remember that a healthy feeling of *remorse* or *regret* is common when a family member dies. *Remorse* carries no implications that your actions prove you are inherently bad or hurtful. It is aimed at the behavior that was done. You choose to live an expatriate life style. *Remorse* can fuel constructive action. It can lead you to take steps to heal any damage your actions of being away caused another person and you can build stronger relationships. *Remorse* is empathy in the face of your pain.

Grief

The evening ritual begins. The sun starts to set and Jack rubs his eyes. As Jack and his mom start the walk down the stairs to his bedroom, she asks him, "What was your day like?"

"Let me think about it," Jack grabs her hand, looks up with big sad eyes and continues the walk.

"How was your day?" she leans over and asks again as he snuggles into his bed.

"Mommy, I had a very *sad* day today. What should I dream about tonight?"

"Dream about what you experienced today," she softly says as she leans closer and smoothes his pillow.

"Mommy, I am thinking about all the people I love in the world and how I feel so lost when someone dies. You say it is *grief* but it is just really, really *sad* for me. I feel like my tears will not stop. I think about how much we love Grandma and how much we will miss her. I am going to dream about how she made me feel special. Mommy, that is what I am going to dream about."

"Do you know how much I *love* you?"

"You *love* me a lot."

"More than you will ever know," she says as she hugs him tightly and kisses him good night.

He just snuggles down in bed pulling the covers up towards his chin.

"Mommy, I am going to miss Grandma. Good night, Mom."

"Good night, Jack, I am going to miss her too."

Optimism

Oxford English Dictionary

1. The actual world is the best of all possible worlds.

2. A disposition or tendency to look on the more favorable side of events or conditions and to expect the most favorable outcome.

3. The belief that good ultimately predominates over evil in the world.

4. The belief that goodness pervades reality.

For a young child: You are jumping for *joy*! You are so *excited* that you know only good things will happen.

Geography

You can experience *optimism* when you visit Duri, Indonesia. The true beauty of Sumatra is not its mysterious volcanic mountains, red sand roads, and lush forest, but the warmth of its friendly people and their *optimism*. This holds true especially when they need to move things from one place to another. It is not uncommon to see 'everything' on the back of a motorcycle moving from place to place, such as a pig ready for slaughter, a large 48 inch flat screen TV, or a two-seater couch. The back of a car (trunk or boot) can be used to carry cattle from one place to another. The local ferry allows carry-on but seeing a man single-handedly carry a king size mattress as his carry-on is amazing.

Duri is a village on Sumatra, an island in Western Indonesia. It is the largest island in Indonesia. Sumatra is not densely populated compared to other parts of Indonesia but it is the fifth most populous island in the world according to UNHCR, the UN Refugee Agency.

Optimism

The evening ritual begins. The sun starts to set and Jack rubs his eyes. As Jack and his mom start the short walk across the hall to his bedroom, she asks him, "What was your day like?"

"Let me think about it," Jack grabs her hand, looks up with a smile and continues the walk.

"How was your day?" she leans over and asks again as he snuggles into his bed.

"Mommy, I had a good day today. What should I dream about tonight?"

"Dream about what you experienced today," she softly says as she leans closer and smoothes his pillow.

"Mommy, I am thinking about how *optimism* is a great trait to have. I am going to dream about those guys we saw today on the street. I wonder how long it took them to decide who had to sit where on the motorcycle. I think the driver must have been a good driver to keep all of them safe on the motorcycle. But the man in the middle must have been very important because he was given the task to keep the wheelbarrow upright and following behind the motorcycle. Yet, the last guy was also important; he had to hold them all together by tightly holding on to the driver's waist. They were so excited and knew they would get the job done. Mommy, that is what I am going to dream about."

She smiles and kisses him good night and says, "Do you know how much I *love* you?"

"You *love* me a lot."

"More than you will ever know," she says.

He just smiles and snuggles down in bed pulling the covers up towards his chin.

"Mommy, I am *optimistic*, I feel this is the best place to be in the world."

"Jack, do you mean Duri is the best place?"

"No, Mom, I mean in my own bed — in my own home — where my family is. Good night, Mom."

"Me too, Jack. This is the best place in the world.
Good night."

Disapproval

Oxford English Dictionary

1. The action or fact of *disapproving*; moral condemnation of what is considered wrong; disapprobation.

2. To prove (an assertion, claim, etc.) to be false or erroneous; to show the fallacy or non-validity of; to refute, rebut, invalidate.

3. To prove (a person) to be untrue or erroneous in his statements, to convict (a person) of falsehood or error; to refute, confute.

For a young child: You don't like what happened. You know it was wrong and it makes you feel bad.

Geography

You can experience *disappointment* in any interaction with peers. This *disappointment* leads you to *disapprove* of how they treat others, including how they treat you. As you move around the world you can have wonderful events and equally sad or disappointing events. Or you or your child will run across a person of whose actions you disapprove. This is especially true if this person's actions cause you or your child to feel *sad* or left out. Moving is not easy and if children and adults are inviting and accepting the transition goes better.

Disapproval

The evening ritual begins. The sun starts to set and Jack rubs his eyes. As Jack and his mom start the short walk across the living room of their full service apartment, she asks him, "What was your day like?"

"Let me think about it." Jack looks up with sad eyes but continues the walk.

"How was your day?" she leans over and asks again as she sits on the edge of his bed.

"Mom, I had a strange day today. I hope I don't have bad dreams tonight."

"What was so strange today?" she softly asks as she leans closer and smoothes his pillow.

"Mom, I am thinking about how I was so *disappointed* today. I am going to dream about what it is like to be the new kid at school and being invited to go to the movies. How excited it made me feel to *belong*. But then the kids left without me. I kept looking at my watch and I was not late they had just left ten minutes earlier than we planned. I was left out. I had no way to reconnect up with them even if I wanted to. Mom, that is what I am going to dream about. I *disapprove* of their actions and I was so *disappointed* that I missed out on fun."

She hugs him tight and kisses him good night and says, "I am sorry you were disappointed. Do you know how much I *love* you?"

"You *love* me a lot."

"More than you will ever know," she says.

"Good night, Mom. Why are some kids so bad?"

"Kids are not bad, they might make bad choices and therefore you disapprove of their choices. Too many bad choices are hard on anyone but especially people who are new to the group of friends. Good night, Jack. I hope tomorrow is a better day."

"Me too, Mom, me too," he says. He moves down in bed pulling the covers up towards his chin. His sad eyes slowly close and I hope that he is able to connect with children who treat others with kindness and respect.

Awe

Oxford English Dictionary

1. The feeling of solemn and reverential wonder, tinged with latent *fear*, inspired by what is sublime and majestic in nature.

2. An overwhelming feeling of reverence, admiration, *fear*, etc. produced by that which is grand, sublime, and extremely powerful.

3. To inspire with *awe*.

For a young child: You can't believe something is so wonderful, it makes your whole body feel 'special'.

Geography

You can experience *awe* when you see one of the most stunning archaeological sites in the world. Angkor Wat takes its name from the Sanskrit word, *nagara*, which means capital and the Khmer, *wat*, meaning temple. Once buried and hidden by the jungle, it has become one of the most widely visited ruins in the world. It is greatly admired for both its grandeur and the guardian spirits that adorn the walls. Angkor Wat is a temple complex in Cambodia, north of Siem Reap.

Angkor Wat is one of the most important archaeological sites in South-East Asia. It contains magnificent remains of the different capitals of the Khmer Empire, from the 9th to the 15th centuries. Angkor Wat temples were always built with symbolism in mind.

As legends have it, Mt. Meru, the residence of god Shiva, is located in the middle of a huge lake. All of the kings of the Khmer Empire considered themselves Devaraja (God King), and so they built residences and temples to reflect their own god-like qualities.

Awe

The evening ritual begins. The sun starts to set and Jack rubs his eyes. As Jack and his mom start the short walk across the lobby to their hotel room, she asks him, "What was your day like?"

"Let me think about it," Jack grabs her hand, looks up with a smile and continues the walk.

"How was your day?" she leans over and asks again as he snuggles into his bed.

"Mom, I had a good day today. What should I dream about tonight?"

"Dream about what you experienced today," she softly says as she leans closer and smoothes his pillow.

He smiles and snuggles down in bed pulling the covers up towards his chin. "Mom, I am thinking about *awe*. I am going to dream about watching the sunrise on Angkor Wat. This morning the temple did look like the home of the gods. I liked the handout that said 'Angkor Wat is made out of an enormous amount of sandstone and virtually all of its surfaces are carved and cause the sun to shine on it with its entire splendor'. Mommy, that is what I am going to dream about."

"Do you know how much I *love* you?"

"You *love* me a lot."

"More than you will ever know," she says as she smiles and kisses him good night.

He just smiles and snuggles down in bed pulling the covers up towards his chin.

"Mom, I loved sharing that national monument with you. I can't wait until tomorrow, when we go on the hot air balloon to see it from the sky. Good night, Mom."

"Good night, Jack."

Contempt

Oxford English Dictionary

1. The action of holding in contempt or *despising*; the holding or treating as of little account, as vile and worthless; the mental attitude in which a thing is so considered (at first applied to the action, in modern use almost exclusively to the mental attitude of feeling).

2. The condition of being held in *contempt* or despised; dishonor, disgrace.

3. An act of disregard or disobedience.

4. To treat as of small value or view with *contempt*; to *despise, disdain, scorn, slight*.

For a young child: You feel bad, your tummy is in a knot. Words do not help.

Geography

You can experience *contempt* in any location in the world where children don't respect the staff members who are employed to help the family in their new location.

Children can easily fall into the patterns of speaking in more commanding tones and less courteous manners to people that are employed in their family to cover some of the parenting roles such as picking them up from school or packing their school lunches. It is important that you explain to both the child and the staff at the same time that the child must be respectful and caring. The caretaker should talk to the child in a calm, firm and non-controlling manner. The expectations on basic human interactions must be kept at a high level so both people feel good about themselves. Often the emotional immaturity of your child leads him to have problems with staff members.

I often think of *contempt* on the same continuum as *resentment* and *anger*. Researchers Ekman and Friesen (1986) say, *resentment* is usually directed towards a higher status individual; anger towards an equal status individual; and *contempt* is directed toward a lower status individual. Remember your child learns his first opinions or reactions from you. How do you treat the staff members in your household?

Contempt

The evening ritual begins. The sun starts to set and Jack rubs his eyes. As Jack and his mom start the short walk across the living room to his bedroom, she asks him, "What was your day like?"

"Let me think about it," Jack grabs her hand, looks up with a smile and continues the walk.

"How was your day?" she leans over and asks again as he snuggles into his bed.

"Mommy, I had a good day today. What should I dream about tonight?"

"Dream about what you experienced today," she softly says as she leans closer and smoothes his pillow. Jack's eyes cloud over and he makes a funny face.

"What's going on, Jack?"

"Mom, I am thinking about all the *contempt*. Why do some kids at school treat their nannies so bad? I saw several kids at school this afternoon be rude to the nannies. I wonder if they are that rude when their own moms or dads are around. I was *embarrassed* about how they just didn't treat them with any respect. Kids can be so awful to people, even adults. Mom, that is what I am going to dream about."

"Jack, how do you treat our driver or nanny? Are you always respectful to them?"

"Yes, Mommy, I am caring and respectful to them all the time."

"Even when I am not around?"

"Yes, always!"

"Do you know how much I *love* you?"

"You *love* me a lot."

"More than you will ever know," she says as she smiles and kisses him good night.

He just smiles and snuggles down in bed pulling the covers up towards his chin.

"Mom, I *love* our nanny because she makes me noodles. Good night, Mom."

"Good night, Jack."

Aggressive

Oxford English Dictionary

1. The quality of being *aggressive*; the disposition to attack others, an unprovoked attack; the first attack in a quarrel; and assault, an encounter.

2. The practice of setting upon any one; the making of an attack or assault on something.

3. Self-assertive, energetic, enterprising.

For a young child: You feel hot and almost *angry*. You won't stop until you win.

Geography

You can experience *aggressive* behavior in a variety of world class sporting events at Leysin. Leysin is located in the Bernese Alps, a group of mountain ranges in the western part of the Alps in Switzerland. It is a lovely Alpine resort that is 1,400 meters high overlooking the Rhone Valley. You can be *aggressive* in the summertime competing in the world cup event of Downhill Mountain Biking. Or you can speed ski down the Alps. Speed skiing is the sport of skiing downhill in a straight line as quickly as possible. It is one of the fastest non-motorized sports on land; the current world record is 251.4 km/h (156 mph). Speed skiers regularly exceed 200km/h (125mph). which is even faster than the terminal velocity of a free-falling skydiver. Snowboard cross, SBX. Boarder cross or BX is a snowboard competition in which a group of snowboarders (usually four) start simultaneously atop an incline course, then race to the reach the finish line first.

Leysin, located in the district of Aigle at the eastern end of Lake Geneva, is a destination for year-around mountain sports and recreation. It is also the home to a number of international schools so you might be *aggressive* towards your studies and come out at the top of your class.

Aggressive

The evening ritual begins. The sun starts to set and Jack rubs his eyes. As Jack and his mom start the short walk across the mountain alpine resort to his hotel room, she asks him, "What was your day like?"

"Let me think about it," Jack grabs her hand, looks up with a smile and continues the steep walk home. When they arrive home, Jack takes off his boots, coat and gloves. He heads into his bedroom and changes into his pajamas. He brushes his teeth and jumps into bed.

"How was your day?" she leans over and asks again as he snuggles into his bed.

"Mom, I had a good day today. What should I dream about tonight?"

"Dream about what you experienced today," she softly says as she leans closer and smoothes his pillow.

"Mom, I am thinking about all the competition we saw on the mountain today. Some of those snowboarders were *aggressive*. I loved watching the freestyle riders. I was so *surprised* to see them using the stairs as a place to snowboard. I hope someday I can be aggressive enough to try jibbing! Mommy, that is what I am going to dream about."

"Do you know how much I *love* you?"

"You *love* me a lot."

"More than you will ever know. I hope you are brave enough to try new things. You can be aggressive but please remember to be safe," she says as she smiles and kisses him good night.

He just smiles and snuggles down in bed pulling the heavy covers up towards his chin.

"Mom, I *love* snow. I'd *love* to go to school in Leysin. I really like the Leysin American School. Good night, Mom."

"Good night, Jack."

Serenity

Oxford English Dictionary

1. Clear, fair, and calm weather; clearness and stillness of air and sky.

2. Tranquility, peacefulness; the state or quality of being *serene*, *calm*, or *tranquil*.

3. Composure, calm, peacefulness, peace.

For a young child: You are calm. Even more calm than when you take ten long deep breaths in . . . and out.

Geography

You can experience *serenity* watching the wheat fields wave over the plains of Kansas. Russell Springs is a small town founded on a beautiful site on the ridge that forms the north side of the valley of the Smoky Hill River. You can see the impressive old courthouse, which is now the Butterfield Trail Museum, from many miles to the south. The wheat fields form a 'sea of gold'. If you are lucky you can see sunflowers growing wild in the edges of the wheat fields.

Russell Springs Museum

Some interesting facts about this town according to the U.S.A. data census (2009) are that there are 27 people living in Russell Springs. The median resident age of these 14 males and 13 females is 56.0 years. The population density is 36 people per square mile and the cost of living index in Russell Springs is very low. It is proud to have the nickname of the Cow Chip Capital of Kansas. The town holds an annual cow chip-throwing contest. Residents collect dried-up cow dung and then hurl these bovine Frisbees. The basic principles of the competition are similar to the more conventional javelin throw. People come from all over the world to compete.

I grew up in Russell Springs, Kansas. One summer, I was sitting on the edge of a wheat field letting the warm sunshine down on my back and watching a small ant crawl across a sunflower. I was free from stress. When I went into the kitchen, my mother asked me several questions. "What were you doing? What took you so long?" I had no idea what to say. I had just spent a nice long afternoon doing nothing. I just looked at my mother and could not think of a thing to say. When you are six-years-old it is hard to explain experiencing the absence of mental stress or *anxiety*. I wish I had known the word '*serenity*'.

Serenity

The evening ritual begins. The sun starts to set and Jack rubs his eyes. As Jack and his mom start the short walk across the farmhouse porch to his bedroom, she asks him, "What was your day like?"

"Let me think about it," Jack grabs her hand, looks up with a smile and continues the walk.

"How was your day?" she leans over and asks again as he snuggles into his bed.

"Mommy, I had a good day today. What should I dream about tonight?"

"Dream about what you experienced today," she softly says as she leans closer and smoothes his pillow.

"Mommy, I am thinking about all the stillness I felt sitting by the side of the wheat field. The air was clean and it was so calm. I could almost hear the sunflowers growing. It was so quiet. It seemed peaceful. Mommy, that is what I am going to dream about. I am going to dream about *serenity.* "

"Do you know how much I *love* you?"

"You *love* me a lot."

"More than you will ever know," she says as she smiles and kisses him good night.

He just smiles and snuggles down in bed pulling the handmade quilt up towards his chin.

"Mommy, I *love* growing things and I like farms with fields. Someday, I will grow a field of sunflowers for you. Good night, Mom."

"I'd love that! Good night, Jack."

Apprehension

Oxford English Dictionary

1. Physical. The action of laying hold of or seizing (physically).

2. *Anticipation* of adversity or misfortune; suspicion or *fear* of future trouble or evil.

3. The faculty or act of apprehending, esp. intuitive understanding; perception on a direct and immediate level.

For a young child: You are *worried*. You don't know what is going to happen so your mind is very busy and you feel *excitement* in your tummy.

Geography

You can experience *apprehension* when you are learning to dive on the world's second longest barrier reef system just off Roatan's shore. Roatan is an island that is 60 kilometers (37 miles) long, and less than eight kilometers (five miles) wide at its widest point. It is located off the coast of Honduras in the Western Caribbean Sea, in the Gulf of Honduras. Roatan has some of the best diving in the Caribbean with spectacular reefs. It is a serene island escape. Professional diving photographers rave about how spectacular the reef is at Roatan.

Apprehension

The evening ritual begins. The sun starts to set and Jack rubs his eyes. As Jack and his mom start the short walk across the beach to their home, she asks him, "What was your day like?"

"Let me think about it," Jack grabs her hand, looks up with a smile and continues the walk.

"How was your day?" she leans over and asks again as he snuggles into his bed.

"Mom, I had a good day today. What should I dream about tonight?"

"Dream about what you experienced today," she softly says as she sits on his bed and smoothes his pillow.

"Mom, I am thinking about my dive trip today. I was so scared at first to be diving so deep. I was worried about my air consumption rate. I was so *apprehensive,* but my dive master made it seem safe. Then I got into searching for fish and looking at coral. It was actually peaceful but still exciting. Mom, that is what I am going to dream about."

"Do you know how much I *love* you?"

"You *love* me a lot."

"More than you will ever know," she says as she smiles and kisses him good night.

He just smiles and snuggles down in bed pulling the light cover up towards his chin.

"Mom, I *love* that we live on the beach and can dive a lot. Good night, Mom."

"Good night, Jack."

Love

Oxford English Dictionary

1. A profoundly tender, passionate affection for another person.

2. A feeling of warm personal attachment or deep affection, as for a parent, child, or friend.

3. Affectionate concern for the well being of others: the *love* of one's neighbor.

4. Strong enthusiasm or liking for anything: her *love* of books.

5. To have a strong liking for: taking great pleasure in: to *love* music.

For a young child: You feel great. You feel special you want to run up and hug the person. You are so *happy*.

Geography

You can experience *love* as you set up a family ritual that you can recreate in any environment in the world. A great ritual is telling your children good night and that you love them.

'Ai' the traditional Chinese character for *love* consists of a heart (middle) inside of accept, feel, or perceive, which shows a graceful emotion.

Chinese love

爱

is

Love

Time goes on. The evening ritual continues.

The sun starts to set and he rubs his eyes. As the Mom and her son start the short walk across the living room to his bedroom, she asks him, "What was your day like?"

"Let me think about it," he grabs her hand, looks up with a smile and continues the walk.

As he jumps into his bed, she sits on the edge of the bed and again asks, "How was your day?"

"Mom, I had a good day today. What should I dream about tonight?"

She leans closer and says, "Dream about what you experienced today."

"Mom, I didn't really do anything special today."

"Every day is special in one way or another. What are you feeling now?"

"I feel warm and comfortable, almost sleepy."

"What is your brain thinking?"

"That I like the fact that I can count on you to talk to me each night and that we have these few quiet minutes together before I fall asleep."

"Jack, I like this time too. It feels special to me."

"It feels like *love* to me. I like that it happens all over the world."

"It is *love*." Do you know how much I *love* you?"

"You *love* me a lot."

"More than you will ever know."

"No, Mom, I know ... I know. I *love* you too. Good night, Mom."

"Good night, Jack."

What have you learned?

Complete the following learning table

Think
When was the first time your child experienced a certain emotion and what was he doing?
1.
2.
3.

Talk

What three family rituals would you like to talk about and discuss with your family?

Apply

What will you do first to start building your emotion stories

Chapter Five

Explaining the importance of emotions to your child

Every word and action from parent to child sends a message. It would be great if we could face every morning with this question:

What are the opportunities for learning and growth today?

Most people assume that an emotion is a feeling that an individual can describe. This ignores the fact the many people have difficulty finding words for their feelings, that feelings are sometimes repressed or distorted, or that people may sometimes deceive others about their true feelings. Children have a hard time reporting their feelings. These facts make it difficult to interpret simple correlations between reported feelings and overt expressions, no matter how accurately the expressions may be measured.

> Boys may have a hard time reporting their feelings. Loyalty is a strong driver for boys. Ask about his group to get more conversation about school.

Children often do not share what is going on in their lives.

"How was school today?"

"It was okay."

"Did you play with someone at recess?"

"Yes."

This type of conversation can go on and on depending on what you ask your child. But at the end of the conversation, you still do not know much about the school day or how your child felt. Parents often report that they never understand enough information about how the school day was experienced.

> ### Significance – Fourth Stage to a Strong Connection
>
> This stage takes the roots of attachment deeper and helps the child feel "connected" and supported by their parents even when they aren't physically nearby. A child needs to feel securely connected and know how precious they are to their parents.

Creating an easy way to share

A mother stopped by my office and said, "I used to know what was going on at school but now that my daughter graduated, my son never tells me anything. I feel so left out."

At all ages, boys seem to bring even less conversation home to their parents. This might be because their parents are not asking them to share information in a way that feels right for them. Boys usually want to blend in. They want to fit in and be part of a group. They tend to play group games and form themselves into structured friendship groups. This need to fit in will dictate much of their social behavior. I encouraged this mom to ask about her son's group of friends and not just about himself.

Some boys wear a mask to protect themselves from being hurt or to portray themselves as a tough guy. This mask can take many guises including 'tough guy', 'cool guy' and 'class clown'. Loyalty is an incredibly strong driver for boys. Boys have a group focus. If you ask about his group you will get more conversation about his school.

If I want information about what happens at school, I would structure the conversation differently.

"What is more fun, math class or the library time?" I ask.

"I guess the math games."

"What did you think or how did you feel, when you were involved in the math games?"

"I think they were fun but my team lost."

Or you can use your son as a consultant on his own life. Instead of saying, "How's math?"

You say, "What did Mrs. Marty teach you today?"

This type of questioning gives your child some guidance on what to talk about but is open-ended enough that your child cannot answer with a "yes" or "no". It is important to realize that your child might not be comfortable about 'feelings and emotions' so it might be hard for him to talk. I always give a child the option to 'think or to feel' so he can share what is most comfortable. If I ask him to just tell me how he feels sometimes this stops the conversation. It might be just too hard to label the emotion.

Giving your child an emotion model

Parents have to listen to their children and help them fine-tune what emotion they are trying to express. One way to encourage your young child to talk about his feelings is for you to do it yourself. Talk about your own feelings. Start by talking in a matter-of-fact way about your own feelings about various activities in your day.

Your goal is to model the use of affective vocabulary and to give your child permission to talk about his feelings. As you go through the day, ask him how he feels about different events.

"When we went shopping today, I felt *sticky* and *miserable* because it was so hot. How did you feel?"

"When Daddy was late for dinner, I felt *sad* that he had to work and a little *angry* because he didn't call us and tell us he would be late."

"When your younger brother does not pick up his toys when I ask him to, I get *frustrated* because I have to keep asking him to do his job."

Encourage your child to go beyond "I like it" or "I feel good about it." Take advantage of opportunities to model use of affective vocabulary. The earlier you start working on emotions the better it is for your child and your family.

Embarrassed, that's me!

> Parents often start too late in building emotional intelligence in their children.

Parents often think they can start understanding emotions with their children once the child has the language to talk about the emotions. I think parents often start too late in building emotional intelligence.

Embarrassment is a common childhood emotion. For many children, *embarrassment* feels like being *scared* so they hate to be *embarrassed*. Also because it is a 'public' event, they are *worried* that the others will remember the event far longer than they should. These situations that cause *embarrassment* can be seen as a growth opportunity or they can be left unaddressed by parents. If you do not talk over the situation with your child, your child is less able to cope the next time something *embarrassing* happens. Usually your child will get *embarrassed* due to two main reasons: they are unable to meet expectations or they lack basic social skills. You need to acknowledge the situation or problem and let your child know that they should try to solve the problem by relying on their own skills. You can say to your child, "You know what to do when this happens, you can rely on your own ability to make the situation better."

Before the age of fifteen months, babies don't seem to recognize themselves as themselves in the mirror. Researchers watched a group of mothers and their babies play in front of the mirror. Next, the moms would pretend to wipe dirt off their babies' faces, but they were putting a small dab of red makeup on the tip of the babies' noses. Then the babies were placed in front of the mirror to see if they noticed the red spot on their noses. Most babies just stared at their reflections and may have found them familiar, but they didn't react any differently when they saw the red spots on their noses. But by twenty-one months, most infants tried to touch or wipe their noses. These babies knew they were the babies in the mirror. The children who touched their red noses in the mirror were the only ones who showed embarrassment. Those who didn't touch their red noses did not show signs of being *embarrassed* (Lewis, Sullivan, Stranger and Weiss, 1989).

Emotions start earlier than most parents believe

The National Scientific Council on the Developing Child, 2004, said children are emotional beings right from birth. It believes that emotions are biologically based and that they are built into children's brains and help them connect to caregivers. The emotions and their development during the first six months of life are mapped in the chart below.

Emotional Development Architecture Brains

Birth	One Month	Two Months	Three Months	Four Months	Five Months	Six Months
Contentment (able to experience pleasure, for example the baby is comfortable)			Joy (shows excitement and happiness, for example the baby smiles when he sees his mom)			
Interest (shows interest in people and environment, for example baby looks intently at his mom's face, eyes, lips)						
Distress (shows irritability) when needs aren t met, for example the baby expresses discontent through his facial expressions and crying)			Sadness (understands the withdrawal of a positive event, for example the baby feels sad when his dad stops playing with him)			Fear From six to eight months,
Frustration (some early forms of anger are experiences, for example when feeding is interrupted the baby may cry or increase the movement of his arms or legs)			Anger (shows irritation, for example the baby cries because he cannot move when he is buckled into the car seat)			

Families have conflict

Conflicts are a normal and natural part of everyone's life. Conflicts are simply the disputes and disagreements that occur between two people. While we tend to think of conflict only in terms of its negative effects, the fact is that conflict can also be positive. Without conflict there is no growth or progress.

> Families have conflict. Understanding others point of view is an essential skill in understanding emotions. Developmentally, it is one of the most difficult concepts to understand.

Understanding others 'point of view' is an essential skill in understanding emotions. Developmentally, it is also one of the most difficult. This is an area where you should think in terms of readiness, not mastery. While young children have difficulty adopting or even identifying the perspective of another person, they can prepare to do so through stories and activities that help them experiment with different points of view.

Point of View

My favorite way to explain this to young children is to stand before the group and pantomime the simple activity of washing windows. I try to get them to think outside the box and I try to elicit several different guesses for my actions. Washing windows might look like waving to a friend. It might look like erasing a white board. I point out that different children saw the same activity differently. This is the same with emotions; the emotion one person is feeling can be different from how you are feeling. The same event can feel different to other people. We all see the world differently. The way we feel about something is called our point of view.

Triggers need to be identified

Children need the opportunity to identify appropriate feelings. They also need to have experience understanding what might trigger certain emotions. The more your child understands why certain things will make his body react in one way or another, the better he will be able to modify any of his behavior if needed. Orally ask your child the following questions: you can note down his responses.

- When someone pushes me, I feel

- When I make a mistake, I feel

- When I do a good job, I feel

- When I help someone and they say thanks, I feel

- When someone calls me a name, I feel

- When someone won't share with me, I feel

- When someone will share with me, I feel

- When someone smiles at me, I feel

- When I get a snack I didn't expect, I feel

Then add to the sentences your own thoughts or examples so you can help build up your child's emotion vocabulary as well as help him see various 'point of view' strategies. The more practice your child has with understanding that emotions are part of the overall situation

and that they vary in intensity, the more of an emotional foundation he will have. Building emotional intelligence insures better family time and more success in school. Expanding the examples above will give you many emotions to think about with your child. Try to make three more additional sentences for each example above.
Example: When someone pushes me, I feel

1. When someone pushes me out of the way so the metal swing does not hit me, I feel _____

_____

_____

2. When someone pushes me down at the top of the stairs leaving school, I feel _____

_____

_____

_____

3. When someone I *love* pushes me out of the way for safety, I feel _____

_____

_____

_____

_____

Work with your child and make up three different situations where each can provoke a different emotion.

1. When I make a mistake _____
    _____, I feel _____
    _____.

2. When I make a mistake _____
    _____, I feel _____
    _____.

3. When I make a mistake _____
    _____, I feel _____
    _____.

Work with your child and make up three different situations where each can provoke a different emotion related to praise.

1. When I do a good job at _____,
    I feel _____
    _____.

2. When I do a good job at _____,
    I feel _____
    _____.

3. When I do a good job at _____,
    I feel _____
    _____.

Work with your child and make up three different situations where each can provoke a different emotion in regard to gratitude.

1. When I help someone _____
   and they say "thanks", I feel_____.

2. When I help someone _____
   and they say "thanks", I feel_____.

3. When I help someone _____
   and they say "thanks", I feel_____.

Work with your child and make up three different situations where each can provoke *anger* or *shame.*

1. When someone calls me _____(a name),
   I feel _____.

2. When someone calls me _____(a name).
   I feel _____.

3. When someone calls me _____(a name),
   I feel _____.

Work with your child and make up four different situations where each can provoke emotions about giving or receiving things.

1. When someone won't share _____
    with me, I feel _____ .

2. When someone won't share _____ .

3. When someone will share _____
    with me, I feel _____ .

4. When someone will share _____
    with me, I feel _____ .

Work with your child and make up three different situations where a smile could make him feel strange or wonderful.

1. When someone smiles _____
    at me, I feel _____ .

2. When someone smiles _____
    at me, I feel _____ .

3. When someone smiles _____
    at me, I feel _____ .

Work with your child and make up three different situations where food is involved.

1. When I get _____

   as a snack I didn't expect, I feel _____.

2. When I get _____

   as a snack I didn't expect, I feel _____.

3. When I get _____

   as a snack I didn't expect, I feel _____.

Let your child add as many different things as they can to the original sentences to build up their emotional vocabulary.

Rituals are important

Children tend to *love* family rituals, even if they don't admit it. Rituals provide a sense of security and can be soothing. A family ritual is anything your family does together deliberately. The routine of whatever you do is what counts. It can be anything. Just make sure you do it consistently.

> Rituals are emotionally enriching. It is never too late to start. Children love family rituals, even if they don t admit it.

Rituals are emotionally enriching. It is never too late to start a ritual. Some children may resist being involved in such rituals. But if rituals are presented in a non-controlling manner and you manage your expectations, all family members will 'get on board' much more readily than you thought. I have worked with many families that want to start building closer family time and sometimes the rituals start with just one person, but if that person feels it is important and keeps trying sooner or later the event can become a ritual.

Let me illustrate this with a story:

AT LAST A FAMILY RITUAL

A family consists of Ted, the father, aged 39, Riki the mother, aged 38, and their three children: a 16-year-old daughter, 12-year-old son and a five-year-old son. The family found out that moving overseas does not give them 'more' family time but they have less time than they have in their passport country. Ted only has free time on Sunday morning because his company has him working Saturdays. Ted wants to connect with his family but everything becomes so stressful on those Sunday mornings. They try to do a Sunday 'breakfast feast' but it causes too much stress. They try to do the trips out to 'Sunday Brunch' but the kids resent the time restraints and the time that they have to be in the car as well as the ongoing morning yells and threats about how they are going to be late. Riki is not into creating any more family time since she spends all week looking after everyone. This is a family in emotional conflict. They love each other but just cannot connect.

We make a game plan to help the family see how important this time is for Ted and how he is willing to take the time to make it work. Every Saturday afternoon or evening Ted sets out a tray with five teacups and small plates. He puts out a snack he picks up from the closest store by his work. It is ready to be opened when someone joins him for a 'coffee break' on Sunday morning. He does not set up a time for this break and he does not make anyone attend. But each and every Sunday morning he reminds his family that he will want a coffee break in about 15 minutes and anyone can join him.

He reports back that he has three lonely Sundays before even one of his children joins him at this first 'event'. They have a nice chat for about 10 minutes over a cup of coffee and a glass of milk. This is 10 minutes more than usual so Ted is excited. Within six weeks, all three of his children join him for their official 'coffee break' every Sunday morning. It gets to where the children pick up special treats on Saturday to put on the tray. I find it interesting that Riki is still not part of the family ritual. When I ask the family how things are going, they are all supportive of the non-stressful connection that they have formed.

"How are you enjoying your family ritual of a morning coffee break?" I ask.

"I love having to stop work to take a break," says the youngest son, Carl.

"Watching videos or cartoons isn't work," says the oldest son as he reaches over and ruffles the hair of his younger brother.

"I really enjoy it. I get to see my kids without competing for screen time or with friends waiting for them to go play, so we actually take time to talk," Ted proudly states.

"We even got Dad to pick up some decent food, after we trained him," giggles the teenage daughter.

We continue the discussion and it is clear that the family is working hard to connect and that they are on the right track. I am worried that Riki is so distant from the 'Sunday coffee break' and does not offer anything to the discussion.

"Do you like the family ritual?" I ask her.

"Yes, it's great for the kids to have time with their dad."

"Why do you choose to not be part of the ritual?"

"Oh, I don't choose to not be apart of it, I just want them to be closer."

"But you are missing out on the connection to your kids and your husband."

The family goes quiet and no one moves at all. Everyone quickly looks at the floor and the playfulness and lightness of the group is gone in just a few short seconds. It takes us a long time to sort out how this made the family feel. Riki thought she was providing a 'special time' for her husband and kids and they felt she didn't want to be part of this family time. We work on the concept of building a 'family ritual' and how the family needs this ritual so they can carry on connecting. This will be important as the children get older and the need to connect is vital. Riki is eager to be part of the ritual when she understands that it is more beneficial as a family ritual and not as a father/child event.

> ### Rituals are Good for Families
>
> - They create a climate of support and security
> - They can provide emotional healing
> - They create a sense of family togetherness
> - They create a structure of shared time
> - They can develop a sense of shared joys and positive memories
> - They can bring humor into the family

Good times create rituals naturally

Most children enjoy reminiscing about good times. Many family rituals are what make up our memories. Talking about the fun times that your children had together in the past can be a great way to help them reconnect. Build these connections when they are young so everyone can stay connected through their teen years and when they go off to college. The family rituals and emotion stories of your family's past will keep siblings connected because they are sharing a common experience. Good memories help eclipse the upsetting ones. It can be a smoothing experience for both parents and children to review past experiences (pictures, video, stories), sharing your emotions to past experiences.

Family rituals create closeness

My family has a series of rituals that we *love*. Some are tied to holidays, birthdays, and special events but some are just around because of their longevity and fun. When your children are expatriates, often parents look for things that might connect their child to their 'home'. Also many rituals can be based around food. We make S'mores. They are a favorite campsite treat for young and old. They are sticky and gooey, and loaded with sugar and carbohydrates. The origin of S'mores dates back to the 1920s. It's believed Girl Scouts first discovered the recipe. S'more folklore suggests that S'mores got their name right by the campfire. After eating one, young kids chanted "gimme some more!"

OUT OF ASHES COME SMILES

We always spend our summers in Lake Tahoe so during this prime campfire time we enjoy our S'mores ritual. But, we don't limit our consumption of S'mores to the campfire. We have them in fireplaces, the dashboards of hot cars, gas kitchen stoves, and microwaves. Jackie is five-years-old. She tries to replicate our ritual all by herself. As the burning marshmallow smell fills our home, we are baffled. No one is cooking in the kitchen. We head out across the house looking for an explanation. I see Jackie sitting on the edge of her bed and notice a black lump of ash on her fingers.

"Jackie, what is that? Why is that here?"

"I wanted a marshmallow."

"Did you ask anyone to help you cook it?"

"No."

"It is a huge mess now. Did you get burnt?"

"No, can I still eat it?"

"Well no, it is just ash. You are lucky that you didn't burn yourself or catch something on fire. How did you cook it?"

"Oh, um."

"You are not going to get in trouble, but can you tell me what happened."

"Um . . . I put the marshmallow on my bed lamp," she looks up at me with her eyes brimming with tears. "For a long, long time."

Kevin enters the room to hear the following discussion.

"Can you tell me why?" I ask.

"I wanted today to be special," she looks around the room not making eye contact with us.

"Special?" I ask.

"I put two marshmallows on the light bulb because I also made one for Grant."

"Why?"

"Because."

"What was special?"

"Today," Jackie states.

We don't want to laugh because it is a safety concern. But it is funny. After a long pause, Kevin and I glance at each other over her head. We want to acknowledge the safety issue and secretly we are proud of her 'scientific approach' to cooking. We wipe off the burnt mess that is all over her bedside lamp. We are not successful; we will just have to throw the light bulb away. Perhaps we can salvage the lampshade? Because we value family time we always make a big deal out of rituals. We find that a five-year-old cooking marshmallows unsupervised on a light bulb is not the best option but it does remind us that family rituals mean so much to children.

> **Recipe for S'Mores**
>
> To make S'mores you need: chocolate candy bar squares, Graham Crackers, and marshmallows.
>
> Instructions: Break off a square of Graham Cracker – add a piece of chocolate. Toast a big marshmallow. Add the hot marshmallow. Top it with another Graham Cracker.
>
> Eat, laugh, and enjoy! Create a family ritual. Not all of your family rituals have to revolve around food but this might be one of the easiest ways to weave rituals into your family routine. You can use holidays or special days as a way to create rituals.

Family rituals can change and evolve over time

Everyone in our family enjoys a second ritual that happens when we are on vacation in Honduras. Almost every evening as the sunsets in Roatan, you will find our family out in the water. We are watching the sunset and are talking about whatever topics might come up. We find that if we are in the warm, clear water we are more likely to stay longer together and listen longer to each other. We sit on some underwater rocks or float around each other. We have a nightly family connection time.

When we watch the sunset from our patio, we will start to prepare dinner, or clean up around the house. Kevin will turn on music and the kids will connect up to the Internet. We get busy and forget to connect to each other.

I didn't move the ritual out into the water, my teenage children did. They say they wanted us in the water so we could spend quality-talking time watching the sunset. It now is something we look forward to daily when we are on holiday there. Because it is a family ritual, when we are on beach vacations during the school year we will also connect as the sun is setting.

Do the Twain

Mark Twain, the pen name for the American author Samuel Langhorne Clemens, known for his novels, *Adventures of Huckleberry Finn* (1885) and *The Adventures of Tom Sawyer* (1876), had a great family ritual. He kept a variety of interesting objects on the mantel above the fireplace. After dinner he would create a new story every night for his children. Some nights it might be about dragons and princesses while the next night it would be totally different. There was always a new adventure with the same main characters according to Gregg Steinberg in *Flying Lessons*.

This would be an ideal ritual for the expat family. Bring out some family souvenirs, place them on an end table or desk, and get your child to create a magical story. Use the same pieces another night, but have him create a new story. After a few weeks, you can use different objects and repeat the process. Let all family members take turns creating new stories with the same artifacts.

Extension activities to try

Some parents want to spend some time doing other emotion activities. I have included several activities to help you expand the work about emotions. Remember many times your children may be more comfortable with a task than you may be as parents. Use some of these suggestions if you want to gain an understanding of the exposure your children have already had to emotions.

Create an **Emotion Words** chart to post in a prominent place. Begin with words that your child wants to put on the chart. Add more words to the chart as they come up during the other activities in this book. As you add words, discuss their meanings. Try to use the words from the chart during discussions about feelings. It is common for a five-year-old to overuse the word *happy*. If you have added words that are similar to *happy* on your chart you can ask him if any of the other words might be a better word choice. I often say, "I understand what you mean when you say *happy*. Is there any other word you might want to use?" If your child is looking at a list that shows *happy, content, pleased, glad, joyful, cheerful,* and *delighted* he might choose a different word to express *happy*.

Make an **Emotion Word Web Chart.** You can build on the activities by creating a web chart. Write the emotion on the paper and draw a ring around it. Have your child brainstorm words related to that emotion. Record each suggestion and draw a line from that word to that emotion. Words that are related to previous contributions can be linked to each other.

Emotion Word Web

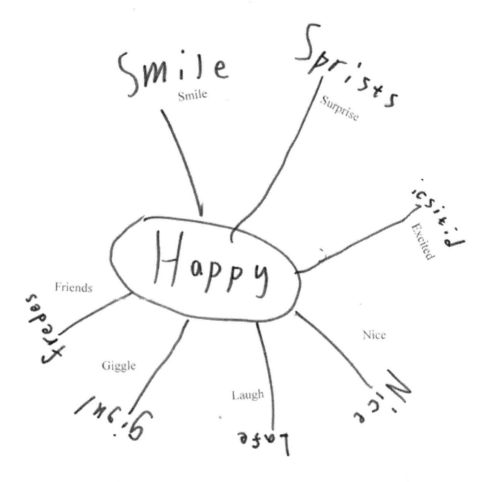

Draw a **WWWWWH chart**. This chart helps your child identify the basic facts about an emotion.

- Who was involved?
- What was the emotion about?
- When did it happen?
- Where did it happen?
- What caused the emotion?
- How did the story turn out?

WWWWWH Chart

WWWWWH Chart

W ho was involved?

Madi, Carla, Trinity and Sonam

W hat was the emotion?

Happy

W hen did it happen?

Begining of year

W here did it happen?

At school

W hat caused the emotion?

They were playing fair and a fun game

H ow did the story turn out?

Then we changed our mind and played another fun game. It was so fun.

Thumbs up, Thumbs down. Look at your emotion story, ask your child to evaluate the story as thumbs up or thumbs down. For each person in the story ask your child what the consequences or outcomes of the emotion might be. Would it be thumbs up for everyone? Thumbs down for everyone? Thumbs up for some and thumbs down for others? Finish the discussion by having your child identify which emotion was the best to put as part of the story title.

Experience it with ***Puppets***. Have your child make stick puppets of the main characters in their emotion story. When the puppets are complete, they can act out the emotion story. Your child could develop a new ending to the story. Sometimes alternative endings can be funny for young children.

Making up Dialogue can be great fun for you and your child. Turn on the TV or a video with high drama. Daytime Soap Operas can be great for this. Pick a show that has two characters on the screen. Then turn off the sound. Begin to make up dialogue. This is a great way to be creative and have fun.

An Emotions T chart helps to identify specific emotional behaviors. Make a big 'T' on the paper (T- chart). Label one side of the paper with the words 'what it looks like' and the other side 'what it sounds like'. Use any emotion you want to explore. Have your child brainstorm specific behaviors for each side of the chart. Change the chart and add a new emotion.

Emotions T chart

Happy	Happy
· Smiles	· laughing / giggles
· laughing	· exetment
· having fun	· playing
	· nice words
	· Warm
What if looks like	What it sounds like

Make an *Emotion Escalator.* Have your child describe an escalator. Draw an escalator on the paper. Explain that when emotions get stronger, we say that people are on an emotion escalator. Discuss an emotion and the levels it can have. Map them on the escalator. It can be fun to see how your child views words that seems similar. Put these words on the escalator: *tired, drowsy,* and *sleepy.* You could also put on the escalator *sad, upset,* and *miserable.* This is a tremendously useful concept to help your child understand emotions and how he has to take responsibility for his behaviors. If I am *sad*, that is okay because we all are *sad* sometimes. If I am *upset*, it is not okay to physically hurt or emotionally hurt someone else because I am upset. If I am *miserable*, I might need help from someone to get some support for feeling so bad. Emotions escalate or de-escalate because of the behaviors of the people involved.

Understanding the ups and downs

Children love escalators so you can easily use them to explain how emotions can vary in intensity and change. Many of the families I see end up with an emotion escalator on their refrigerator. I set up the story with these examples:

"Do you ever go on those moving stairs in a big building? We are going to look at these six emotions and see how they work with each other. Let's make this our 'ground floor'. You are on the ground floor. Here are six emotions that are in ABC order. Let's put them on the emotion escalator."

The child receives these words on individual index cards, *anxiety, comfort, confidence, discomfort, hope* and *worry*. I read each word as I hand it to him.

"Make them into two piles. You will have one group that is going down the escalator, things you worry about or things that bother you".

Use the exact word *'worry'* so this can guide your child since this is the first time he has been introduced to the emotion escalator. Watch him shuffle the cards and answer any questions he has about the words. Work together to show how on the ground level you can choose to go up to *comfort* or move down to *discomfort*.

Going down, you find after discomfort comes *worry* and then *anxiety*. When you are back on the ground level, you can head up to *comfort* again and then you can get to *hope* and move on up to *confidence*. Use words that imply you have a choice in which way you move and to take ownership of your own emotions. Children love to move the index cards around. Some children even take small dolls to travel up and down the emotion escalator. One child colored the lower levels red and the upper levels green. She made a colorful flower garden on the ground level and a rainbow on the top floor. She got this example and personalized it.

> Children need to take responsibility for their own learning. They need to know that if they lose interest in a class they slip into feeling indifferent then they can easily fall into boredom. This impact on their learning is driven 100% by their own attitude.

When I talk about their 'learning' in class I use five emotion cards: *boredom, curiosity, fascination, indifference, and interest*. It is important to highlight to your child that when he is feeling *indifferent* during a school lesson he has to be very careful to not slip down into *boredom* because this means he is switched off learning. I had a young girl yell out across the crowded playground, "Ms. Julia, I was *indifferent* but I didn't go to *boredom*." She was a very proud five-year-old that was struggling learning her native language. She had mastered English but was behind in her home language and found these classes hard to be focused in. She knows that from ground level she can get to interest, curiosity, and fascination with just a little effort. This is where true learning takes place.

Working in a school, 'learning' is always an important focus so we also think about how *frustration* then *confusion* and on up to *puzzlement* puts us on the ground level. When we go upstairs we get *insightful* on up to *enlightened* and then the top floor is *euphoric*. These are hard words for many children, but through using the emotion escalator they really understand them and enjoy learning new ways to express how they are feeling.

Awe can be a hard emotion to explain. Start with *terror* at the lowest level. Move up to *dread*. Then travel up to *apprehension*. You are on the ground floor. Now move up to *calm*, then up to *enchanted*. The next level up is *enthralled*. The top floor is *awe*.
Your child might need to work on the emotions involved with being *embarrassed*. Some times he might think this is the 'worst day' possible or that the worst event has happened. It is important for him to understand that there are so many things he does well; getting him to label the things he does on this emotion escalator will help him get a better perspective on his actions and his emotions.

Start the discussion on ground level. When things go well you are *content*. *"What things are you doing when you are content?"* Let your child talk about these positive things. Then move on up to *pleased*. Again discussion is important. *"When you feel good about yourself what things are you doing when you are pleased?"* Many parents jump to the 'hurtful or embarrassed' event and this does not help a child's self-confidence. You need to do some build-up first on good feelings. The top floor is *prideful*. This does not have to be public pride or boasting. This means taking pride in what you are doing and how special it makes you feel. *"What do you do that makes you proud?"*

Going down the escalator it is important to add *chagrinned* so your child understands that often he is *angry* about being let down. Then *embarrassed* comes on the next level. *Humiliation* is on our lowest level. Some children will add other levels and words as they try to understand their own emotions. I always let any emotion they bring up stay on our emotion escalator. I make sure that they have it on the level they want and can explain how one emotion leads to another emotion because of some action or event.

"Children always look to their parents. Parents should be more calm. You can teach children that you face a lot of problems but you must react to those problems with a calm mind and reason. I have always had this view about the modern educational system: we pay attention to brain development, but the development of warmheartedness we take for granted."
 – Dalai Lama, Time July 5, 2010

CCK's -Cross Cultural Kids

What have you learned?

Complete the following learning table

Think

When was the first time your child experienced a certain emotion and what was he doing?

Talk

What three family rituals would you like to talk about and discuss with your family?

Apply

What will you do first to start building your emotion stories?

Chapter Six

Taking Action – activities for your family's emotion stories

This is a workbook for your family to use in order to explore your own emotion stories and to explore and create memories. This is a working book with spaces for you to collect your child's thoughts and words.

> *"If you want your life to be a magnificent story, then begin by realizing that you are the author and everyday you have an opportunity to write a new page."*
>
> Mark Houlahan

Feel free to do these worksheets in any order

Supporting your child's understanding

The meanings of words are given not only by explicit definitions but also by identifying related words or synonyms. To understand a word like *anxiety*, it is useful to know related words, such as *fear, worry, concern, dread, uneasiness,* or *apprehension*. If your child is having trouble understanding an emotion it is helpful to give him the opposite words. In this case, I would use *bold, calm,* and *confident* as antonyms for *anxiety*.

> It is vital for young children to understand the situation so they can connect the emotion to their own past experiences.

Some parents want to use photographs of the places in which their emotion story took place. This is an easy way to set the stage but still photographs reveal little or nothing about the situation in which the family finds itself. Make sure you set the stage with what the location was like or what the situation was like before you decide on the exact emotion this story will be about. The situation is information people usually need to judge the likelihood of an emotion being present. It is vital for a young child to understand the situation so they can connect the emotions to their own past experiences.

Think in terms of readiness as well as mastery. Many emotions or concepts are difficult for young children. You child might not be ready to master this skill or concept. They are able to work at a readiness level, which will prepare them to master the emotion when they are older.

Getting started

Create a verbal story. This is great way to explain what you want to do with emotions. If your child needs structure you could write on a large piece of paper the following items:

- Character one
- Character two
- The place
- The activity or action
- The problem or conflict they need to solve
- The emotion
- Something they need to find or discover

Take all suggestions. As a parent it is a good idea if you start the verbal story. Say a sentence with one of two of the names or descriptions that are on the paper. Then ask your child to add to the story. Continue until you have covered everything on the page. Starting verbally allows you to decide which emotion fits best with which location and story.

Three young six-year-olds came up with this story:

- Character one – He is a small boy with black hair and black eyes. He is funny.

- Character two – This is the mother she is nice and friendly.

- The place – They are coming to school but the car is broken.

- The activity or action – Learning how to ride on the back of a motorcycle in Bangkok.

- The problem or conflict they need to solve – To use one motorcycle or two?

- The emotion – Upset (no car) scared (mom) happy (boy).

- Something they need to find or discover – Money but easy, mom has her purse.

This is their story:

The car is broken. We can't be late to school. Mom is mad. We are upset. We wave to the motorcycle man to come over. We don't know if one motorcycle or two motorcycles will get us to school. We get two. Mom is scared. The boy is happy. Mom tells driver to go real slow. Boy laughs as his motorcycle speeds away. He is very happy.

Use full sentences and many descriptive words when talking with your child. Listen when he talks, and expand on what he says. This will give him the chance to hear and to practice new words.

Best reasons for telling and sharing stories

Children *love* stories. Hearing interesting stories about family members or friends helps children feel more connected to those around them. Children *love* to hear stories about when they were younger as well as stories about when their parents were little kids. If your child gets stuck working on an emotion, take that emotion from your own childhood and expand on it so he sees the rich language and expressions of your childhood event.

To really connect with your child share how you felt when you were his age. The more complex an emotion is the more likely it is that you might need to share that emotion from your own childhood so your child understands.

Sometimes the more complex an emotion is the more likely it is that you might need to share that emotion from your own childhood for your child to understand. Also it allows you to make a connection with your child if he can empathize and thus understand how you felt when you were his age. Your child can develop better listening skills and learn to ask questions during story times. Your children hear new words as they listen to stories, which can help build their vocabularies. Children who hear lots of stories learn how stories work. They learn that characters solve problems and how stories begin and end. This helps them understand other stories they will read later in their school years.

Things to avoid when working together

Working with your child should be a positive experience. Don't ever force your child to read or write with you if he doesn't want to. If your child begins to think of reading or writing time as a negative experience, he will try to find ways to avoid it. Both of you will miss out on wonderful book time. Parents often overestimate the amount of time that their child will focus and work on a project. I always tell parents that age is the factor at which you need to look carefully. If you can catch a good minute or two per birth year, then you are successful. Your three-year-old would be interested and involved for about three to six minutes. Your five-year-old would ideally work between five and ten minutes on this project. Never expect to get a compete emotion story done at one sitting because it is the process of revisiting the event and emotion that makes it become part of your child's emotional vocabulary and emotional intelligence.

Let me demonstrate how to use the workbook with a story:

This is a small part of our conversation. Grant and Jackie are working on building an emotion story. They are looking at the 'joy' page of the workbook.

"We want to work on 'joy' for our emotion story," calls out Jackie.

"Yes, we talked about it last night with Daddy," states Grant.

"Where is your emotion story going to take place?" I ask.

"We wanted to do Australia, where we were born," Grant reaches for a crayon.

"But that was joy for you and Dad but not really for us," states Jackie, "so we decided to talk about our trip to Monkey Mia, where I had fun."

"Is that okay for you, Grant?"

"Yes, it will be fun," he comments.

"Grant, who is going to be the people in your emotion story?"

"There is just you and Jackie in the story, I am still a baby to be born and Daddy is working."

"What activity is going on?"

Jackie is quick with her words, "We are on the beach wading with the dolphins."

"Was there a problem or a discovery?"

"This is where I get to be part of the story or memory. The story is about a dolphin about to have a baby and you are about to have me," says Grant.

"So the emotion you both connected to was joy?"
Grant jumps in, "If I was swimming with the dolphins, I'd be so happy, so yeah, it is joy."

"Are there any other things about this event that you could put in the story?" I ask.

"Let's put in where we stayed on the beach, let's talk about the hotel," says Jackie.

*"Let's remind people about the mommy dolphin I saw in our photos,"
says Grant.*

We take time discussing what the words will be in the story and how
we can expand some of the thoughts. We check to see if we have all
the areas of the workbook completed for the page 'joy'.

*"Let's talk about how we are going to illustrate this story. Will we
have one picture or will each of you draw your own? What titles or
captions will we add to the story?" I ask Jackie and Grant.*

*"I want to draw my own picture," states Grant holding a blue
crayon.*

"I want to draw the camp area and ocean," says Jackie.

*"Okay, I will go get some more paper," I say as I set out another
box of crayons to prevent any concerns about sharing as they work
together.*

Some families will be able to produce one story and one illustration.
Other families will be more successful if each child is responsible
for their own story and illustration. There is no right or wrong way to
work on creating your family's emotion stories. I have had families
that start out each making their own versions at first. Then, as they
work closer together, they end up making common stories later on
in the workbook.

Experience - *joy*

Be as concrete as possible. It's easy to start talking about *joy* in abstract terms, but this goes over the heads of young children. Discuss *joy* in terms of specific actions and objects, and then move to more abstract aspects, such as motivation or point of view. A young child would understand the *joy* of a birthday cake and birthday party, but they might not understand the *joy* of a new baby who has not arrived into his family yet or into his household.

Where is your emotion story going to take place?

_____

_____

_____

_____

_____

_____

_____

List the people in your emotion story

_____

_____

_____

_____

What activity is going on?

_____

_____

_____

Is there a problem or conflict they need to solve or is there something they need to find or discover?

_____

_____

_____

_____

_____

_____

Any other comments about this story?

_____

_____

_____

_____

Illustrations are a wonderful way for your child to connect to something and it allows him to take more ownership of the story. But not all children like to draw; some prefer words. I always give children the option to either write or draw their emotion story. But it is important for them to put captions or titles on their pictures so you can have a visual clue in writing about the story.

Draw your *joy* story or add more to your *joy* story.

Experience - *surprise*

Make an effort to share lots of stories with your child, whether it's family stories with real-life situations or make-believe stories with imaginary characters. Your child will *love* them even if you start with a short five-sentence story and build your way up to longer ones. Don't worry about creating a 'masterpiece'; your child will be a great audience.

Where is your emotion story going to take place?

_____

_____

_____

_____

_____

List the people in your emotion story

_____

_____

_____

_____

_____

What activity is going on?

_____

_____

_____

_____

_____

_____

Is there a problem or conflict they need to solve or is there something

they need to find or discover?

_____

_____

_____

_____

_____

_____

Any other comments about this story?

_____

_____

_____

_____

Draw your *surprise* story or add more to your *surprise* story.

Experience - *anticipation*

Make the stories fun and interesting! Follow your child's interests and he'll likely want to create more and more stories.

Where is your emotion story going to take place?

_____

_____

_____

_____

List the people in your emotion story

_____

_____

_____

_____

_____

_____

What activity is going on?

_____

_____

_____

Is there a problem or conflict they need to solve or is there something they need to find or discover?

_____

_____

_____

_____

_____

_____

_____

_____

Any other comments about this story?

_____

_____

_____

_____

_____

_____

_____

Draw your *anticipation* story or add more to your *anticipation* story.

Experience - *fear*

Everyone knows what *fear* is. Anyone who has been in an accident or has been threatened by someone bigger or more powerful has most possibly felt *fear*. Our language probably has more synonyms for the word *fear* than for any other emotion term. It causes sweating, rapid heart beating, and trembling. You can feel butterflies in your stomach, or be scared stiff. *Fear* is a powerful emotion.

Where is your emotion story going to take place?

_____

_____

_____

_____

List the people in your emotion story

_____

_____

_____

_____

What activity is going on?

_____

_____

_____

Is there a problem or conflict they need to solve or is there something they need to find or discover?

_____

_____

_____

_____

_____

_____

Any other comments about this story?

_____

_____

_____

_____

_____

_____

_____

Draw your *fear* story or add more to your *fear* story.

Experience - *anger*

Anger is an emotion that almost everyone feels at one time or another. It can generate an impulse to retaliate, attack, or injure the source of the provocation. Blanchard and Blanchard, *Aggressive Behavior* (1986), carried out a survey in Hawaii with several thousand college students, finding that a few situations seem to trigger most angry reactions. Verbal or gestural insults are a form of challenge found in every culture. *Anger* occurs when individuals perceive a challenge to something they regard as symbolically or actually belonging to them or to a group with which they identify. Challenges to the angry individual's authority, independence, image, or control are the situations that trigger the most anger reactions.

Children need the vocabulary to talk about their feelings in times of conflict, and they need to be able to identify the triggers that evoke those feelings. They also need to be able to identify the degrees of intensity of feelings, particularly of *anger*. These skills and understanding take time to develop, and this is an area where it is useful to think in terms of readiness. For many people, learning to handle their feelings in conflict is a lifelong endeavor.

Where is your emotion story going to take place?

List the people in your emotion story

_____

_____

_____

What activity is going on?

_____

_____

_____

Is there a problem or conflict they need to solve or is there something they need to find or discover?

_____

_____

_____

Any other comments about this story?

_____

_____

_____

_____

_____

Draw your *anger* story or add more to your *anger* story.

Experience - *disgust*

Help children see cause and effect. Young children need to understand the relationship between cause and effect, a relationship that is central to understanding the emotion *disgust*. When discussing actual or hypothetical situations with children, help them to see the whole problem and how specific actions and behaviors contributed to it.

Where is your emotion story going to take place?

_____

_____

_____

_____

List the people in your emotion story

_____

_____

_____

What activity is going on?

_____

_____

_____

_____

Is there a problem or conflict they need to solve or is there something they need to find or discover?

_____

_____

_____

_____

_____

_____

_____

Any other comments about this story?

_____

_____

_____

_____

_____

_____

_____

Draw your *disgust* story or add more to your *disgust* story.

Experience - *trust*

Children *love* to be the main characters of the stories, so make up stories where your child can be the star. If they don't want to be the star, a favorite pet, stuffed animal, or sibling can be the main character.

Where is your emotion story going to take place?

_____

_____

_____

_____

List the people in your emotion story

_____

_____

_____

_____

What activity is going on?

_____

_____

_____

_____

Is there a problem or conflict they need to solve or is there something they need to find or discover?

_____

_____

_____

_____

_____

_____

Any other comments about this story?

_____

_____

_____

_____

_____

_____

Draw your *trust* story or add more to your *trust* story.

Experience - *sadness*

All childhood experiences provide opportunities for a child to understand *sadness*: a friend won't play with you, a pet dies, and a toy is lost. For expatriate children often it is when a friend moves away. As parents, you would like your child to learn about *sadness* in small doses. You hope that living through each of these small experiences will prepare him to face the larger inevitable sorrows that come with the deaths of grandparents and, eventually, parents.

Where is your emotion story going to take place?

....

....

....

....

List the people in your emotion story

....

....

....

....

What activity is going on?

_____

_____

_____

_____

_____

Is there a problem or conflict they need to solve or is there something
they need to find or discover?

_____

_____

_____

_____

_____

_____

Any other comments about this story?

_____

_____

_____

_____

_____

Draw your *sadness* story or add more to your *sadness* story

Experience - *acceptance*

Emotions are the glue that is binding people together. Conversely, emotions are also what drive people apart. If you can get young children to be accepting of others, society will benefit as a whole. *Acceptance* is a person's agreement to experience a situation without attempting to change it, protest or quit.

Where is your emotion story going to take place?

_____

_____

_____

_____

_____

What activity is going on?

_____

_____

_____

_____

_____

Is there a problem or conflict they need to solve or is there something they need to find or discover?

_____

_____

_____

_____

_____

Any other comments about this story?

_____

_____

_____

_____

_____

_____

_____

_____

_____

_____

_____

Draw your *acceptance* story or add more to your *acceptance* story.

Experience - *grief*

Caring parents don't push children to learn letters or become 'real readers' before they are ready. The journey to literacy begins with positive interactions with you. The journey to understanding loss begins with positive parent interaction when the child is ready. This holds true for the emotion *grief;* not all children are ready to make a story about *grief.* Some children have not experienced *grief* or they cannot connect to it, while other children will eagerly want to do this story.

Where is your emotion story going to take place?

_____

_____

_____

_____

_____

List the people in your emotion story

_____

_____

_____

_____

What activity is going on?

_____

_____

_____

_____

Is there a problem or conflict they need to solve or is there something they need to find or discover?

_____

_____

_____

_____

_____

_____

Any other comments about this story?

_____

_____

_____

_____

_____

_____

Draw your *grief* story or add more to your *grief* story.

238

Experience - *optimism*

At certain points in the story stop and ask your child questions to
encourage his positive emotion involvement. Add a song or a joke.
You can use rhyming words. As your emotion story takes form,
keep it interesting and look for other ways to engage your child's
point of view. *Optimism* is having the tendency to take a favorable
or hopeful view. Does he usually expect the best? Or is he more
"If something can go wrong for me, it will"? Asking such questions
will help your child understand his affirmation of his *optimism*.

Where is your emotion story going to take place?

_____

_____

_____

_____

List the people in your emotion story

_____

_____

_____

_____

_____

_____

What activity is going on?

_____

_____

_____

_____

Is there a problem or conflict they need to solve or is there something they need to find or discover?

_____

_____

_____

_____

_____

_____

_____

Any other comments about this story?

_____

_____

_____

_____

_____

Draw your *optimism* story or add more to your *optimism* story.

243

Experience - *disapproval*

Children often feel *disapproval* directed at themselves or from them towards others. *Disapproval* goes hand in hand with disappointment. Childhood is full of disappointment. As loving parents, you hate it when your child feels *sad* and you will almost always jump through hoops to help him not cry.

You force older children to play games with him; you force younger children to leave his toys alone. You let him stay up late even if you know it not good for school tomorrow. You even buy him toys he can't live without. You justify your actions and even manipulate things just so you do not have to disapprove of your child's actions. Learning how to deal with disappointment is developing a vital skill of learning how to adapt. Your child needs this ability throughout his whole life. As parents, you need to help him sort out his feelings when it comes to disappointment and how to pick himself up and try another plan. If you disapprove of his action, you need to tell him.

Where is your emotion story going to take place?

_____

_____

_____

List the people in your emotion story

_____

_____

_____

What activity is going on?

_____

_____

_____

_____

_____

Is there a problem or conflict they need to solve or is there something they need to find or discover?

_____

_____

_____

_____

Any other comments about this story?

_____

_____

_____

_____

_____

_____

_____

Draw your *disapproval* story or add more to your *disapproval* story.

Experience - *awe*

The easiest way for a young child to experience *awe* is to experience *wonder*. As he bends down to watch the water roll off a grass blade, give him time to *wonder*. Inform him that when something seems so special, it is called *awe*. When you experience something that is breathtaking, tell your child. Use words to describe how you feel and tell him that another way to say this is *awe*.

Where is your emotion story going to take place?

_____

_____

_____

_____

_____

List the people in your emotion story

_____

_____

_____

_____

What activity is going on?

_____

_____

_____

_____

_____

Is there a problem or conflict they need to solve or is there something they need to find or discover?

_____

_____

_____

_____

_____

Any other comments about this story?

_____

_____

_____

_____

Draw your *awe* story or add more to your *awe* story.

Experience - *contempt*

Contempt is universally understood in both Western and non-Western cultures (Ekman and Friesen). It is an expression in which the corner of the lip is tightened and raised slightly on one side of the face (or much more strongly on one side than the other) to signal *contempt*. This is why a young child will often be quick to respond, "I was just joking or I was kidding." They want us to fall for the smile when in fact they were being derogatory to another person.

Where is your emotion story going to take place?

_____

_____

_____

_____

_____

_____

List the people in your emotion story

_____

_____

_____

_____

_____

_____

What activity is going on?

_____

_____

_____

_____

_____

_____

Is there a problem or conflict they need to solve or is there something they need to find or discover?

_____

_____

_____

_____

_____

_____

Any other comments about this story?

_____

_____

_____

_____

Draw your *contempt* story or add more to your *contempt* story.

Experience - *aggression*

If your child is feeling frustration do you intervene? Do you say that you are doing that out of *love* and caring? Are you preventing him or her from learning about adaptation? If so, you are setting your child up to want circumstances to change just for him. He will learn to make demands and then if he does not get what he wants he will become aggressive. He might even grow up to be an adult who cannot cope when he gets disappointed. As parents, you need to add to your children's internal reservoir of self-confidence and resourcefulness.

Where is your emotion story going to take place?

_____

_____

_____

_____

_____

List the people in your emotion story

_____

_____

_____

_____

_____

_____

What activity is going on?

_____

_____

_____

_____

_____

Is there a problem or conflict they need to solve or is there something they need to find or discover?

_____

_____

_____

_____

_____

Any other comments about this story?

_____

_____

_____

_____

Draw your *aggression* story or add more to your *aggression* story.

Experience - *serenity*

Once in a while, be creative with your child. Build a blanket fort and get a flashlight and listen to the quiet night together. Or softly read a book to your child in the bathtub. You live in a wondrous world that is also rushed, competitive, and tiring. You ask too much of yourself. You can feel frazzled. Routines help; even older children flourish when there are rhythms to the day, every day. Build in some quiet time. Talk less; you often overload your children with long explanations that veer between the confusing and the boring. Talk less and listen more. Sometimes over-talking is a symptom of your own *anxiety*. Give your child time and opportunity to look in long, slow detail at the natural world. Let him experience calm. Quiet. Peace. All of this is *serenity*.

Where is your emotion story going to take place?

List the people in your emotion story

What activity is going on?

_____

_____

_____

_____

_____

Is there a problem or conflict they need to solve or is there something they need to find or discover?

_____

_____

_____

_____

_____

Any other comments about this story?

_____

_____

_____

_____

Draw your *serenity* story or add more to your *serenity* story.

Experience - *apprehension*

It is important to get children to stay 'in their bodies' instead of letting them disconnect and intellectualize when they are *apprehensive* about something. I encourage them to point to the part of their body where the feelings are happening. It is important that your child can connect to 'how his body feels'. This often gives him the words to explain it to you. A child that is very upset might say, "It is very scary and dark in my head". I would encourage him to tell me the colors he sees or feels in his head. "It is grey (*sad*) and some black (*angry*) feelings," he might explain.

Where is your emotion story going to take place?

_____

_____

_____

_____

List the people in your emotion story

_____

_____

_____

_____

_____

What activity is going on?

_____

_____

_____

_____

_____

Is there a problem or conflict they need to solve or is there something they need to find or discover?

_____

_____

_____

_____

_____

Any other comments about this story?

_____

_____

_____

_____

_____

_____

Draw your *apprehension* story or add more to your *apprehension* story.

Experience - *love*

Author and lecturer Leo Buscaglia was judging a contest to find
the most caring child. The winner was a four-year-old child whose
next-door neighbor was an elderly gentleman who had recently lost
his wife. Upon seeing the man cry, the little boy went into the old
gentleman's yard, climbed onto his lap, and just sat there. When
his mother asked what he had said to the neighbor, the little boy
said, "Nothing, I just helped him cry". Young children are full of
compassion and *love*.

Where is your emotion story going to take place?

_____

_____

_____

_____

_____

List the people in your emotion story

_____

_____

_____

_____

_____

What activity is going on?

_____

_____

_____

_____

_____

_____

Is there a problem or conflict they need to solve or is there something
they need to find or discover?

_____

_____

_____

_____

_____

Any other comments about this story?

_____

_____

_____

_____

Draw your *love* story or add more to your *love* story.

> "There are five qualities or abilities that help a youngster move towards adult life with the resources needed to find their passion, manage the obstacles that may get in their way and persevere towards making their dreams come true: resilience, self-respect, problem solving, visioning and gratitude."
>
> – Susan Stiffelman, Parenting without Power Struggles

What have you learned?

Complete the following learning table

Think

What three emotions were the hardest to connect to or recall?

1.

2.

3.

Talk

What stories would you like to talk about and share with others? Why?

Apply

What tips will you share about working with your child?

Chapter Seven

Tying it all together - developing your family plan

How to get everyone in the family involved

Each family will have to make stories that work for their family. I ask families to take the parts that work for them or the parts they connect to and start what I call a 'family plan' to help them to build emotions. In *Actual Minds, Possible Worlds* (1986), Jerome Bruner argues that while we may learn about the physical world through logical rules and abstract principles, we learn about the social world through narratives.

> *"There are two stages on which we live our lives: experience and the retelling of that experience."*
>
> – Susan Engel, The Stories Children Tell

I *love* working with families on their emotion stories. To the family, this is an exciting experience. The children usually *love* the memory they want to share. The parents are deeply touched by this as well as recalling the actual event. We start the process orally and then take written notes; the story crystallizes the personal meaningful aspects for the storyteller and listeners alike.

An emotion story is a story that may be repeated again and again, and some day your child may even repeat it to his children. As time passes, each family member may develop his or her unique version of the story. It is a family story. I *love* to see how your three-year-old's version might be the simplest response, but is a building block for the child to understand what he is trying to convey to others. When your family takes this version and expands on it, a very real story is made.

> We learn about our world through logical rules and principles; children learn about their social world through stories.

The easiest way to get the whole family involved in building a story is to ask different members to take on tasks to help build the story. You can have a 'title generator' for the person who wants to get involved but does not have enough time. You could ask an older child to come up with 'higher level' thinking words to expand on the story. An adult could help color in a picture that a child draws. The goal is to make this quality family time. Some emotion stories are revisited so often that they become stronger and have much more meaning for the family members.

Write emotion stories in your own language

Is there a common denominator or shared belief for emotion words in other languages? Emotion concepts are organized according to a circular structure, a 'circumplex', in a two-dimensional space of pleasure and displeasure and degree of emotion. When I work with families who speak different languages, I always wonder if they will judge the emotions in the same way as I do as an English-speaker. Sometimes you do have to define what you mean as you go along, and clarification is vital. There are several key studies which pinpoint how this seems to hold up worldwide.

> Third Cultural Kids need to express themselves in any language that gives them the most powerful feelings. Validation of how they feel is vital.

1. Russell (1983) used 28 emotion terms with native speakers of Chinese, Japanese, Croatian, and Gujarati; he found that in all cases circumplex orderings hold true but with some differences in the exact placement of each term. Russell used a category and sorting method specifically designed for testing circularity. All of his data yielded nearly identical circular patterns. These 28 emotion terms were common for four very different cultures.

2. Data collected by White (2000) among the Cheke Holo people of the Solomon Islands was similar to what Russell had discovered. Now, five different cultures viewed basic emotions in the same way. They came up with 15 words that were then grouped according to similarity of meanings. These clusters resulted in a circumplex result. Emotions are best described in this two-dimensional space or shape because of their complexity.

3. Dario Galati (2008) used emotion terms from Italian, French, and Spanish. This resulted in a different number of terms in each language: 84 in the Italian study, 108 in the study of French, and 86 terms for the study of Spanish. All of the results showed a similar circumplex. These three languages also grouped emotions into basic categories that were similar.

4. Heider (1991) collected data on the emotion language of three cultures from Indonesia, Minangkabau, and Java. Bahasa Indonesia is the national language of Indonesia and Minangkabau and Javanese are regional languages that are spoken by different ethnic groups in the country. They came up with 229 words for emotions and produced a cluster map of 44 different clusters. One of Heider's conclusions following this study was "The words used for emotions are significant data but they are not necessarily the only or the best way to get information about emotions."

Human behavioral measurement

Some people have never heard of the concept of a circumplex. It is often used to measure human behavior. It can be viewed as merely a useful pictorial representation. A circumplex is viewed as implying circular order. This shows that variables that fall close together are more related than variables that fall further apart on the circle. Children understand how things falls on a circle, but some children prefer to see a list that implies the order of words being similar or more related. They find it easier to 'see' this list located on page 304.

These body reactions are interesting to know. And the fact that they are similar reactions around the world is fascinating. These studies caused many researchers to expand their focus on emotions. They wanted to now look at what exactly the body does when various emotions are experienced. They wanted to see if these body changes would be different depending on the age of the human.

Worldwide study on how people of all ages feel

A study by R. Plutchik and H. Kellerman, in *The Measurement of Emotions* (1989), was conducted on the frequent reactions that different emotions cause in humans. Their results found some universal actions. They took 2,235 people from eight countries and studied their body responses when faced with different situations, and monitored their emotions. They used people of all different ages and categorized their emotional responses. They wanted to see if there were some common traits in all emotions regardless of the age of the person. These are their findings:

- The emotion *joy* causes the reactions of feeling warm, faster heartbeat, muscles relaxing, laughing, smiling, and moving forward, lengthy utterance, speech disturbances.
- The emotion *anger* causes the reactions of heartbeat faster, muscles tensing, change in breathing, feeling hot, changed facial expression, change in voice, moving against, lengthy utterance, speech tempo change.
- The emotion *disgust* causes the reactions of silence, changed facial expression, lengthy utterance, muscles tensing, withdrawing.
- The emotion *sadness* causes the reactions of crying, sobbing, lump in throat, withdrawing, heartbeat faster, muscles tensing, feeling cold.
- The emotion *fear* causes the reactions of heartbeat faster, muscles tensing, perspiring, change in breathing, feeling cold, changed facial expression.
- The emotion *shame* causes the reactions of silence, heartbeat faster, feeling hot, changed facial expression, withdrawing.
- The emotion *guilt* causes the reactions of silence, heartbeat faster, lump in throat, muscles tensing.

> Children can describe their heartbeat, how their brain feels, if they are hot or holding tension. Parents just need to ask the right questions to understand their child.

Young children are honest. If you ask them to describe how their body feels when they have a certain emotion, they will think hard and search for words to tell you how they feel. They will describe their heartbeat, how their brain feels, if they are hot, or where they are holding tension. If you take the time to ask, you will soon see how your own child really does feel when he is experiencing certain emotions.

MOMMY, ARE YOU LISTENING?

We move to Jakarta, Indonesia when Grant is six months old. We move into a home that is far too big for a family of four and a dog. We quickly acquire two cats and a host of workers that came with the house. We have 24-hour security so this results in four full-time guards; these four men rotate shifts so someone is always in the front of our house and garage area. We have two full-time live-in maids who are nannies/cleaners/cooks. We also have a gardener and a pool man that show up on some unknown schedule. Our two children have a lot of outside influence in their lives. They are surrounded in a language-rich environment of Bahasa Indonesia.

Grant is now three years old and Jackie is six years old.

It is the second night in a row that I have to stay late at school for parent-teacher conferences. When I get home the house is clean, dinner is made, and the kids are ready for bed. I am tired but content and happy that things are as good as this.

"Grant, it is time to go to bed, get a book and let's go," I say after giving both kids a big hug.

"Mom, Jackie is staying up later?" Grant questions with an unfair ring in his voice.

"Yes, but it is your story time so let's go."

Now that Grant is three we have a well-established bedtime. It starts with Grant getting a book of his choice, a short snuggle, and then lights off. Then Jackie gets a book of her choice, a short snuggle, and lights off. Then I get my own time. This usually takes 15 minutes per child so I look forward to my own time after a long hard day at work. As I tuck Grant into his bed, he starts to squirm and pulls at his tee shirt. I continue to read his story but his pulling becomes more and more intense.

"Grant, what is going on?" I question.

"Ketiak," he quickly replies.

"Ketiak?"

"Ketiak." More pulling on his tee shirt results in his face becoming more and more upset.

I run a smooth hand across his chest and give several more hugs. But he just keeps repeating this word. I call Jackie to come into the bedroom to see if she can translate this Bahasa Indonesian word for me. She cannot. I call my husband in to be my translator; he does not know 'ketiak'. Now the easy 15 minutes has grown into over 30 minutes.

"Grant, help me; what other word can you use?" I urgently ask again.

"Jahat." This is his second choice of words to help explain the problem.

The three of us look at Grant and then look back at each other. 'Jahat' is a term we know because we see it often in the newspaper. It is used to explain the corruption of political opponents in the country. Most parents hate to admit that their three-year-old has them stumped. It is even harder to have to go to the nannies' door and knock after they have the evening off to ask for help with your three-year-old.

We have a 10-minute discussion on if we should go get our staff. Then we have a five-minute discussion on who will go ask for their help. We deem that Jackie will be the perfect one to explain our 'confused' issue to the staff and ask for help. I am too embarrassed to go. Down the stairs, Jackie trots to get a staff member to help us.

My husband and I with Jackie, two maids, and one security guard gather around Grant's bed. The mystery word is reviled. Armpit! Yes my son has an itch in his armpit. This 'need' takes six people and over an hour to understand. It is then quickly dealt with. A quick dab of antiseptic lotion and Grant is in bed and ready to go to sleep. I have only one more story and snuggle to go before my evening is my own time. It is 75 minutes later than normal.

This is a good example of parents not listening to the real needs of their child. If we had just attended to his needs our bedtime would have been much earlier for all of us. We got stuck on the 'language' of the situation instead of the issue or concern. Grant was miserable with an itch in his armpit. You need to take time to listen to your child. False assumptions can lead to miscommunication.

Understanding your child

Infants can produce almost all of the discrete facial movements that adults produce, but the capacity to inhibit these expressions does not appear until middle childhood when frontal lobe development is complete. In simple words, this means our preteens and teenagers will have the ability to not react or show emotions if they do not want to show them.

Faces are important. Most people are strongly influenced by, and interested in, the face. You keep pictures of other people's faces on your desks and on your walls. Faces of great men and women are often photographed and enlarged to gigantic proportions. Faces are important for your infant. Due to his eyesight development, the optimal distance you should hold your face from his face is seven to 10 inches or about 18 to 24 centimeters. Parents are very good at showing an infant their facial expressions because they have to hold the baby close when they feed him or rock him.

Faces are very important. Encourage your child to understand how his own face feels and how his face changes as his emotions change.

As a child gets older, a parent seldom allows the child to focus directly on the parent's face to see how an emotion is expressed. Things just happen. You need to encourage your child to understand how his own face feels or how his face changes as his emotions change. Ask him to tell you how your face changes when your emotions change. He knows exactly how to describe his angry dad's face or his disappointed mother's face. I worry about children who are unable to do this because it means they have not had enough contact time with their parents or they are not able to read the social cues of the people they are closest to. If he can't read these clues from loved ones, he will not be able to read them from his peers. School will be a hard place for him to understand what is going on.

Conflict between crackers and broccoli

Many parents want to keep their child way from conflict. Most parents will do anything to keep their children from causing conflict with their siblings. I *love* conflict because I see it as a positive way to grow. Conflict allows great discussion. Conflict with young children allows them to experience a wide variety of behaviors and get support to understand how to make good choices and actions.

Research by Repacholi and Gopnik, (1997) *Early Reasoning about Desires: Evidence from 14-18-month-olds,* talks about a creative experiment, using crackers and broccoli. Researchers showed 14-month-old and 18-month-old children two different bowls of food. One bowl was filled with Goldfish crackers and one was filled with raw broccoli. When given the choice between the two foods, both the 14-month-olds and the 18-month-olds chose the crackers.

Next, a researcher tasted the food in front of the children. When she ate the crackers, she made a disgusted face and said "yuck." With the broccoli, she smiled and said "yum." Then, with both bowls of food in front of her, she put out her hands and asked the babies to give her some food.

The 14-month-old babies gave the researcher crackers, even though she said "yuck" when she ate them before. They didn't yet understand how another person could want or prefer something different from their own tastes and desires.

The 18-month-old babies gave the researcher broccoli, showing that despite their own preference for crackers, they understood that the adult preferred the vegetable. They understood that the adult had different desires for food. 18-month-old children are beginning to understand that people are truly different. They knew what they wanted was not necessarily what the adult wanted.

> We often underestimate the knowledge that our children really do have when it comes to emotions.

When I encourage families to start early with emotion work, they often feel their child is too young to understand. Studies like this prove that you often underestimate the knowledge that your child does have. This is what causes confusion or conflict. Your child needs to learn how conflict works and how to resolve it.

Recognizing visual cues from your parent

All children read their parents' faces to see how they are doing. They might be talking at a family dinner or reunion and quickly look over to see if their mom or dad is watching them. They are checking to see if they are getting a frowning face, squinted eyes, or raised eyebrows signaling that a parent wants them to 'stop talking'. Children are great at getting a certain glance or stare and knowing exactly what their mom or dad is saying even if no words have been spoken. Your child reads your visual clues from an early age.

Sorce, Emde, Camps and Klinnert's (1985) research with children created a 'visual cliff' – a Plexiglas covered table that had a deep end that seemed unsafe to cross. As they crawled over the table to get a toy, the babies reached the 'deep end' and weren't sure whether they should keep going. At this point, the babies looked at their mothers while the researcher studied what the babies did.

The mothers and babies were divided into two groups. As each child approached the visual cliff, the mother smiled, created a happy face, and, using only her facial expressions, encouraged her baby to cross the table. The second group of mothers also placed the toy at the deep end of the cliff, but as their babies moved closer to the 'edge' these mothers showed a fearful face, again without talking or using their hands to add to the communication.

When the mothers posed a fearful expression, not one of the babies ventured across the deep side. But almost all of the babies who saw their mother's happy face crossed to the deep end. These babies recognized their mother's expression and decided what to do based on what they read in their mother's face.

As parents, you owe it to your children to give them honest verbal and nonverbal communication about your own emotions. You also have to be careful that you do not pre-censor an activity or event that your child might enjoy or grow from with your facial responses when your child is telling you about this new option. In seconds, you can change how the child feels about an event, new toy, or new food. This is especially true of anything that puts us out of our comfort zone or our dislikes. In schools a common concern is how a parent views her child's new teacher. If the parent is not supportive or positive about the teacher, the child will quickly stop investing as much energy in learning.

Do we benefit from screen time?

I am always torn between the benefits of the computer or screen time and the isolation it can cause for some children. Some children have the ability to engage with the computer, shut it off and socialize; other children will get involved and forget to come up for air. I do, however, like the research that computers have allowed us to really understand what a child is experiencing. This is due to their ability to simulate humans and record the interactions. Two excellent studies are worth noting:

Computer generated facial expression ('morphs') have contributed new insights into the meaning of facial expressions.

1. In one, photographs of real faces of six basic emotions, *happiness, sadness, fear, anger, disgust* and *surprise* were compared with computer synthetic images. It was found that the real faces were judged somewhat more accurately than the computer drawings (Wehrle, Kaiser, Schmidt and Scherer, 2000).

2. To illustrate how subtle variations in head position and orientation may influence judgments of emotions,

Lyons (2000) used Japanese Noh Masks held in different orientations; these were compared with a human face in comparable positions. When the masks were titled forward it was often described as happy. A mask with a backward tilt was often judged as sad.

Caretakers and screen time

Children imitate what they see on the screen , even if it is background noise. As caretakers of these precious people, we need to be very careful of what they are exposed to in their daily lives.

Most children watch a lot of television, videos, and screen games. Babysitters and caretakers often use television and videos as an activity to occupy your child, and the television frequently remains turned on during other home activities. Parents always want to know if their child imitates what they see on the 'screen' even if it is background noise. Yes! In Barr and Hayne's (1999) experiment they checked to see if babies would imitate what they saw on a screen. Of the 120 children, aged 14 months and 24 months, half (60) watched a 20-second video of a stranger on television playing with a new toy. The toy was made of two cubes attached by a small tube, so it looked like a small dumbbell. On the video, the person pulled the toy apart in a special way three times, showing the children an action to copy. The remaining half of the children (60) was split into two groups. One group did not see any video, and the other group watched a stranger on television playing with the toy without taking it apart.

Here is what happened. With the 24-month-old children who saw the video, 18 out of 20 (90 per cent) took apart the toy just like the person on television. Of those who didn't see the person playing with the toy, only four out of 20 (20 per cent) took apart the toy on their own. This is a clear indication that two-year-olds can learn from watching someone on television.

One group of 14-month-old children did not see the toy again for 24 hours. Even with this delay, eight out of 20 (40 per cent) remembered and imitated what they saw the adult do with the toy. Only two out of 20 (10 per cent) took the toy apart on their own. This research shows that children as young as 14-months-old will copy some of what they see on television, even if the person they are watching is a stranger. In this research, in just 20 seconds of watching TV, children as young as 14 months learned how to do something new. Think of what they might see in one hour of TV. Additionally, as children get older, they get better and better at imitating what they see (Barr and Hayne, 1999).

As screen time becomes more intertwined in our lives, the impact of its pluses and minuses needs to be carefully monitored.

Emotion knowledge adds protection

With the increase in screen time and online connections in your child's daily life, it is important that he knows what he is feeling and how to communicate those feelings to an adult that he *trusts*. This is a real concern. There is excellent work being done in criminal justice systems and child protection agencies around the world, which are trying to combat this issue and keep your child safe. Organizations like the Child Exploitation and Online Protection Centre (CEOP) consistently research and apply that knowledge to understand how young children use the Internet, and the problems and risks they can face on the Internet.

I feel the first line of defense is your own child's ability to know when something just does not seem right and he gets an *upsetting* feeling. He knows his own emotions and feelings so he can inform you if he feels '*gross*', '*uncomfortable*' or '*nervous*' when he is online. Your child needs to know who to talk to if he or she is *worried*. Your child needs to know what to do if he or she is ever *scared* or *unhappy* about something online.

Your child's narratives hold keys to support him

Each time a child describes an experience he or someone else has had, he constructs part of his past. This adds to his sense of who he is.

Every story your child tells, acts out through play, or writes contributes to a self-portrait. Each time your child describes an experience he or someone else has had, he constructs part of his past, adding to his sense of who he is and conveying that sense to others. Each time your child makes up a story about something that might have happened to himself or to another, he expands his world.

Children who include emotions in their writings at home or in school are often more in touch with their own emotions and understand how one person's emotions might affect another person's emotions. Younger children can illustrate what they are feeling or what their story is showing. Sometimes an event that seems totally trivial to you remains indelibly imprinted in the mind of your child.

> Children who include emotions in their writings are often more in touch with their own emotions and understand how one person's emotions might affect another person's emotions.

A study by Warren, Emde, and Sroufe (2000) is interesting. Five-year-old children were asked to complete 16 stories based on brief initial statements. The following are some examples of the initial statements:

1. In a park, the child kicks a ball away from the family. Suddenly a scary dog appears and barks loudly.

2. It's nighttime and the child is alone. Suddenly the lights go out, and the child thinks he/she hears a monster.

3. The child has been looking forward all day to visiting with a friend, but Mom tells the child that he can't go.

Warren et al. concluded that children who tell stories indicating difficulty in separating from parents and who are unable to seek help from parents might be at risk of later anxiety. Children often include things that worry them in their journals or school writings. In classrooms where children have encouragement to add emotions into their stories these children are more vocal and honest about how they are feeling.

The more exposure your child has to including emotions in his daily vocabulary, writing, or speech, the easier it is for him to understand how his choices affect others in his environment.

What this means for older children

Listen carefully to how your teenager describes him or herself. If he describes himself as shy or gloomy he is implicitly telling you something about the primary emotions that go to make up those traits. Shyness, for example, implies frequent feelings of *fear*. If your teenager says he is dark or gloomy, this implies frequent feelings of *sadness*.

Children in the sixth and seventh grades who were identified as depressed were aware not only of the *sadness* they felt but also of their simultaneous feelings of *anger*. Plutchik stated that eight out of 10 depressed children would say that depression is a combination of *sadness* and *anger*. He feels by age 10 children can recognize that emotions can be mixed, and most children can draw pictures expressive of basic emotions including *depression*.

> A five year old understands how his actions affect others and how certain choices he makes will affect different people in different ways.

Children as young as four draw pictures that express their basic emotions. By the time your child is five, he can easily discuss and draw emotions if he has had exposure to these emotions. A five-year-old can also understand how his actions affect others and how certain choices he makes will affect different people in different ways.

RUN, BOY, RUN!

Two five-year-old boys are talking about their ongoing concerns in the playground. Both boys feel that they are part of the problem but not the cause of the problem. I step in to help them and to clarify a few points.

"What choice did you make?" I ask.

"I hit him."

"What choice did he make?"

"He ran away and didn't play with me."

"Do you want to go talk to him?"

"Yes."

"What would you say?" I ask.

"Don't run away from me when we are playing."

"I thought he ran away because you hit him."

"But we were playing."

"What does it look like to play nicely with a friend?"

We have a discussion on what playing looks like and how it feels when someone plays nicely with you. We talk about what other choices he could have made before he 'hit' the other boy. We talk about what people do when they get hurt. We even cover how no one wants to stay around to get hit again. The boy decides to go and talk to the other boy, but instead of being mad at the boy for running away, he is going to ask him to play with him again. He is going to say he will not hit him. I hope the second child is willing to give this young boy a second chance. He has a plan of action.

Having a plan is a good idea. Developing your 'family plan' is unique. The classic idea behind this workbook is growth. There are wonderful advantages in having a guide to help with family interactions. The principles that are applied in this workbook are effective for encouraging family growth and good communication. There is no one 'Father knows best' family or classically normal family. Every family is human and subject to human errors and emotions. When your family discussion begins, try to remember that what one person considers positive may not always be seen in the same light. This is a positive exercise meant to build respect and communication as well as reaffirmation of the family's worth. Sometimes many surprises can be found and shared.

Three unique family plans

Families are eager to show their emotional growth.

BEING LEFT

Nan (26) is a single mother of two young girls. Vicki is four-years-old and Tari is six-years-old. They have been on two back-to-back overseas assignments as a family of four but recently their father moved out. They are living in an area without any family support but are coping. We are meeting to see if they can find more emotions to feel. They are all feeling loss and sadness. We start talking about emotions and the ones they might want to explore. We have already had two meetings on 'moving on' and in this session we are going to focus on memories.

"We are going to brainstorm some memories; you call them out and I will write them on the white board. Everything goes and then we will talk," I state.

Nan opens the brainstorm session with, "Sadness."

Tari says, "Scared."

A quiet fills the room and we sit in silence.

In a small quiet voice Vicki says, "Can I add happy?"

"We are going to add all the emotions that your family has had so 'happy' sounds perfect," I comment and add 'happy' to their list of emotions.

Their list grows to have these emotion: sadness, scared, happy, grief, mad, tired, left out, angry, upset, lonely and unhappiness. I stop them when we get to ten emotions on our list. I ask each family member to carefully look over the list and come up with the emotion that is most important to her. This is where we are going to start. I give each one a small sheet of paper and ask them to copy the emotion they want to do first. I help Vicki write her word 'happy'. I collect the papers and mark on the white board the three tally marks.

"Happy gets one mark," I say as I tally up Vicki's response.

"That was my choice," says Tari.

Nan laughs, "Mine also."

"Yes!"

This very sad family has just decided that happy was the most important emotion to start with in building up their emotion workbook.

Without being open to exploring all of the possible emotions, this family might not have moved from *sadness* on to a more positive plan. With some emotional healing they will be ready to work on the other emotions on their list. Since this family needed to expand their memories of good and bad times, I decide to help them set the following family plan:

- Week one – at home think of the one event where all three are *happy*. Come up with the location, who is in the story, and what is going on. Each person will draw her own memory of this event.

- Week two – list six other words that mean *happy* and come up with times the family has these experiences. Create the location, who is in the story, and what is going on for all six emotion words. It is okay to be a family of three or recalling memories when they were a family of four.

- Week three – start working through the workbook on emotions. We will draw names out of a hat to see who gets to pick the first emotion story to build on in the workbook. We will also draw for the second place to pick the second emotion page to work on. We will continue to fill out the emotion workbook and if the family decides to skip or not complete an emotion that is okay.

WE LOVE OUR BORING LIFE

The Anders family consists of four members who are on their first overseas assignment. Daisy is the mother, aged 36. Darren, the father, is 40-years-old. Harry is six-years-old and Carla is eight-years-old. They are in my office trying to cope with changes in schools, new culture and all the things that are different from being in the U.S.A. They are adjusting well but feel the new job and new school are not giving them enough family time. When I suggest that they might want to create emotion stories for quality family time the kids get excited. Daisy seems to be somewhat interested but Darren is not very interested.

"Emotion stories are a great way to connect and do an activity without any pressure, and they can cause real family time," I repeat.

"We haven't even been to any place special yet," states Darren.

"We just moved to Indonesia and haven't been out of Jakarta," confirms Daisy.

"Emotions take place all over the world and especially in our homes," I remind them.

I ask the children to tell me about Texas. What do you do for fun there? What activities do you go to? Where did you go for fun? As the children talk, I put their words up in a word web connecting words to events and people to places. Darren and Daisy just watch and do not add anything to the discussion. After ten minutes, I have enough information to start creating a complete workbook, but the parents need to be ready to support the children with this project.

I make an outline of how to help them and we come up with this family plan:

- Today – we will copy down all the information on the white board to keep as a reference. We will vote on the 'one emotion' that seems most interesting. I will walk you through how to do this emotion in the workbook and clarify any questions.

- Next week – we will see if you liked completing the emotion story and decide what to do next.

The family comes back to my office. Darren is holding a typed story. Daisy has a bag full of glittery markers. Harry has a large construction paper full of drawings and Carla has a small diary. Each family member is eager to share his or her contributions to the "Anders Emotion Stories".

Harry says, "We had to get a huge paper 'cause Texas is so big!"

Carla proudly opens her diary, "I added much more to our story and made it into a short story; it is part fiction and part real."

"I still feel we haven't been to any place fancy or special so I got 'special' markers so we could really decorate up our poster," adds Daisy, holding out the bag of markers.

"I knew I wouldn't like this, it seemed like a waste of time. We are all so busy but I gave it a try on Sunday afternoon with the kids. It works," says Darren. "Daisy and the kids were all excited over the markers so I thought I might as well join them."

"This is a wonderful collection. What will you do with the poster?" I ask.

"We had to take it down off the wall of the dining room,"
says Harry.

Darren is quick to add, "It helps the empty house
look better."

"Can you tell me about the typed story?" I ask Darren.

"I decided that we can't just plan ahead to do all the things we are
going to do, but we must also think about what we have already
done. We had nine years as a family in Texas so a large part of our
life is Texas. I am making the children's stories into computer form
so I can send it back to the family in Texas."

"What are you calling your stories?"

"I don't know. Maybe 'Harry's and Carla's Texas Thoughts'?"

"Are you and Daisy involved in this process?"

"Um . . . yes."

Daisy jumps in, "Let's call it 'Amazing Anders Tales and
Travels'."

Darren is the first to reply, "Yes, we could add any travels we do
from Jakarta and really keep the family up to date."

The family sits and ponders this. A lively discussion follows on who
is going to do what for next week and what 'tale' or emotion they
should cover next week. Sadly that week, Daisy calls to tell me that
they will not be able to keep their appointment and she will get back
to me. It is six weeks later and I still have not heard from Darren or
Daisy. I see Harry and Carla around school and they appear happy
and healthy so I don't ask them about what we had done earlier in
their relocation to Jakarta.

The week before we head off for the Christmas holiday, I find a large package on my desk. Inside is the "Amazing Anders Tales and Travels" hot off the press with a small card that displays a tropical Santa with black flip flops or slippers instead of boots on the beach. Darren has written, "This has become our family ritual, we are adding to our book after each trip or event that we want our extended family to know about. Merry Christmas."

CAN WE COME IN?

A familiar face is outside my office door knocking. My door is open so this is strange. I go to the door see how I can help this person. She is a teacher at my international school. Alongside her are her husband and two children, aged four-years-old and six-years-old. They all say at the same time, "Can we come in?"

They need to talk about how they can't balance their family time with work commitments and how each child keeps saying, "It's not fair". We discuss all the issues that seem to get in the way of their family having good quality time together. We agree that having something structured to do is better than having all their time spent on trying to figure out what to do and disappointing everyone. It had gotten to the point that often when they had free time they just wasted the time with everyone doing their own thing and not even really interacting. They have a three-day weekend coming up so we make a family plan that looks like this:

Thursday: Make a copy of the weekend and plan family time that is not negotiable or changeable. I suggest that they go for thirty-minute work time and to have it associated with a normal meal plan so it did not add more stress getting everyone back together in the same room.

Dad said, "Let's do it first thing right after breakfast."

"Do you eat breakfast all at the same time on the weekends?" I explored.

"No," the family all respond.

"How about lunch?"

"We can," Mom says, "if I just don't break down and get the kids' food when they first demand it."

I get reassurance out of all four family members that they will eat lunch at the same time on this Saturday, Sunday, and Monday. We create a unique family plan.

Saturday:

1. Read the eight primary emotions stories in the workbook. This should only take about fifteen minutes. Do not read the dictionary meaning or the geographical information page.

2. Have each family member verbally answer these questions. Which was your favorite story? Of these eight emotions, which one do you know best? Which one is the hardest to understand? The youngest in the family goes first and no one can add or comment until he is finished. Continue so everyone has a turn. Thank each other for taking time to be together and go back to your regular plans. You have added thirty minutes in your day off, but it was quality family time.

Sunday:

1. Meet again at lunch. This time make an oral story of your own emotion. Each person picks one of the eight emotions and makes his own story. This time you start with the oldest person. Hearing adults (mom and dad) share their stories first will help your children share later on. Also there is no pressure to 'make' anything or create something that feels like homework. Having everyone follow the same guideline helps each child feel like it is fair.

Monday: (Holiday)

1. Parents share that everyone is going to a big hotel brunch on this holiday. We agree that time before lunch will be much better than time after lunch. Being in the car is an ideal time to do more 'family connection' time.

2. Dad is driving so Mom gets to pick one of the ten emotional dyads. She reads the story. Each person comments on what they thought of the location, event and emotion. We start with Mom first to answer, then Dad, and then oldest child.

3. The task today is to tell a story that happened to you when you had the same emotion that Mom just read about. This time the order to share is Dad, Mom, youngest child, and then older child.

Teachers use a technique called modeling to help students learn a new skill or get better at an already acquired skill. It's easier for most people to imitate something they've seen than something they have heard described. This is why I often ask Mom or Dad to go first in sharing.

Some families need an outside person to just lay down the ground rules to make the kids stop arguing. Fair is not always equal. This is an important thing for children to learn. There are benefits of being a mom and dad. You can go first. I always encourage parents to let their children know the 'rules' of something prior to the event so there is less to argue about. But I never feel parents should be the gatekeeper or the scorekeeper to remember who is to go next. It is your children's responsibility to keep track and decide how this is going to work. "When you figure it out, let me know" is a great sentence for a parent to remember. Don't get involved in things that don't matter to you. Do you really care who goes first, who sits where, or who has a car window?

Each family is unique so therefore their emotion stories or workbook will be unique.

Don't get stuck on doing it the 'right way'. Listen to your children and just get started. Don't get bogged down in endless debate or discussion on one emotion, just move on to another one. Try to create a whole picture of positive emotion growth and cherish the good moments.

List of circumplex words

Start circle here	Continue with Row Two
Accepting	Remorseful
Agreeable	Hopeless
Serene	Depressed
Cheerful	Worried
Receptive	Disinterested
Calm	Grief-stricken
Patient	Unhappy
Obliging	Gloomy
Affectionate	Despairing
Obedient	Watchful
Timid	Hesitant
Scared	Indecisive
Panicky	Rejected
Afraid	Bored
Shy	Disappointed
Submissive	Vacillating
Bashful	Discouraged
Embarrassed	Puzzled
Terrified	Uncertain
Pensive	Bewildered
Cautious	Confused
Anxious	Perplexed
Helpless	Ambivalent
Apprehensive	Surprised
Self conscious	Astonished
Ashamed	Amazed
Humiliated	Awed
Forlorn	Envious
Nervous	Disgusted
Lonely	Unsympathetic
Apathetic	Unreceptive
Meek	Indignant
Guilty	Disagreeable
Sad	Resentful
Sorrowful	
Empty	
Continue to second list of words	**Continue to third list of words**

Continue with Row Three	Continue with Row Four
Revolted	Wondering
Displeased	Impulsive
Suspicious	Anticipatory
Dissatisfied	Boastful
Contrary	Expectant
Jealous	Daring
Intolerant	Curious
Distrustful	Reckless
Vengeful	Proud
Bitter	Inquisitive
Unfriendly	Playful
Stubborn	Adventurous
Uncooperative	Ecstatic
Contemptuous	Social
Loathful	Hopeful
Critical	Gleeful
Annoyed	Elated
Irritated	Eager
Angry	Enthusiastic
Antagonistic	Interested
Furious	Delighted
Hostile	Amused
Outraged	Attentive
Scornful	Joyful
Unaffectionate	Happy
Quarrelsome	Self-controlled
Impatient	Satisfied
Grouchy	Pleased
Defiant	Generous
Aggressive	Ready
Sarcastic	Sympathetic
Rebellious	Content
Exasperated	Cooperative
Disobedient	Trusting
Demanding	Tolerant
Possessive	
Greedy	

Continue to fourth list of words	Continue back to first list of words

What have you learned?

Complete the following learning table

Think

What thoughts or reflections do you have about this section?

Talk

What assumptions have you made that have led to miscommunication?

Apply

What will you apply and turn into a habit?

Chapter Eight

Dealing with hard emotions with your own children

Parenting is hard enough when everything goes as planned. It is so much harder when your child doesn't have social skills to fit in or finds it hard to make friends. Sometimes it is hard to admit that your child has a problem. Some children make poor choices, behave in cruel and unethical ways, and /or are on the receiving end of both. As parents, you have to get out of denial and help your children.

Why anger is a hot topic

Many children don't have the proper language skills to use in getting their angry feelings out. They may know some of the appropriate words, but they're not clear on how or when to use them. Children need to understand that a person's *anger* almost always affects others. They need to learn that it is hard to walk away from, or ignore, someone who is angry. But they need to learn that it's almost always better to do so.

Your child needs to understand *anger* as an emotion or feeling. *Anger* awareness focuses on helping children be cognizant of their angry feelings. Body language is important to children. When people talk about their *anger*, they tend to stiffen and turn away from to whom they are speaking.

If your child learns to understand the *anger* behind his actions, thoughts, and feelings, he can learn to control and use it in constructive ways. Likewise, if he has an advocate who is willing to discuss the *anger* and help him work through it, he may be better able to handle similar situations in the future.

Expressing *anger* is difficult, especially for children. Even when *anger* is expressed in a constructive way, the angry person risks making the other person angrier with him. *Anger* has to be expressed with the ultimate goal of improving the relationship and moving on. Instead of a 'who's right and who's wrong' altercation, the resolution should focus on what can be learned from the situation at hand.

Understanding Anger

- Children need to understand that it's okay to get angry.

- Children need to recognize that anger is a normal feeling.

- Children need to realize that something good can evolve from an angry situation.

- Children need to accept help in managing their anger.

I'M NOT ANGRY, I'M MAD

Jackie and Grant are playing on the floor with a variety of toys. They are peacefully building a Lego town and a car area but they are not playing together. They are just occupying the same space of the living room floor.

"Can I help?" said Grant.

"No, you might mess up something" Jackie replies.

"No, I won't."

"Yes, you will."

"But I can build you a great car wash."

"I already have a car wash."

"No you don't."

"Yes, I do."

"Can I see it?"

Jackie picks up a small part of her Lego town and shows him reluctantly.

"Can I play with it?" Grant asks.

"No, it is part of my town."

"Can I help?"

"No"

"You never let me play!"

"That's because you always mess things up."

This could so on and on. As a family, we are lucky; seldom do Jackie and Grant explode into *anger*. They are not destructive towards each other. Nor do they do mean things on purpose. This might be because they are three years apart in age, or the fact they are different genders. I might just be a lucky mother. Who knows!

But this type of constant ongoing bickering is just as destructive to a family. When it gets to the level where it is a no win for both children an adult has to step in. I feel that parent intervention has to be quick and before things become 'hurtful' to either child. This works well with my children.

"Okay, let's quiet down and talk about this. Grant, are you angry?"

"Yes."

"How angry?"

"Really angry!"

"How does it feel to be really angry?"

"I feel bad."

"Tell me how your body is feeling."

"I feel like I want to kick something. My heart is pounding too fast."

"And your face?"

"My face feels red and hot."
"Would it be okay to hit Jackie or to kick her toy town?"

"No, I guess not."

"Why?"

"I could hurt Jackie and get into trouble."

"You are right; it is not okay to hurt someone in our family."

"Jackie, how do you feel?"

"I'm not angry, I'm mad."

Parents' interactions will usually be to try to stop their child from feeling angry or mad. You need to actually have him label how angry or mad he is. Then try to get your child to talk to another peer using 'I messages'. It is important to help your young child master the 'I message' technique.

I - Messages

I feel _____ when you _____
because _____ please _____.

If your child is having trouble coming up with these 'I statements', you can model it or you can start the 'I message' and have him finish the sentence. In this story there are many different comments that our children could have made. It is important to help them understand that they need to be clear on what they need and how they feel.

"Grant, I hate it when you try to help me when I don't want your help because it makes me feel mad and I don't want you to do it anymore," Jackie says.

"Jackie, I hate it when you are mean to me because it hurts my feelings and I want you to be nicer to me."

"Okay," stated Jackie.

"Okay," Grant parroted back.

"Sorry I was mean to you."

"Can I help fix your town?"

"No, not now."

"Really?"

"Yeah, it's okay. Just be careful."

Sometimes children do not end an argument as you might have planned out in your mind. What is most important is to see if they are able to continue to work with each other. Jackie and Grant were not actually playing together prior to the problem so it is unrealistic to think that they might get angry and then make up and start playing together. Sometimes things are going great in a family when a group of family members can be in the same area and enjoy each other's company without interacting.

Body and impulse control is important

Body control is important when understanding *anger*. Physical violence is a natural reaction to *anger*, but it is never acceptable. Exploding in *anger* might get the desired result in the short run, but it doesn't resolve the problem. Your child must learn that it is not okay to hit others to make his position known, just as it is unacceptable to threaten or intimidate others with force.

Self- Regulation Awareness

Control anger when things don't go as planned and focus on controlling what you can control

- Refrain from hurting the feelings of others when angry.

- Delay your responses to anger until you calm down.

- Use deep breathing to calm yourself

Impulse control is important when understanding *anger* in children. When children are *angry*, it's hard for them to control their natural impulse to hurt others in an effort to make themselves feel better. It's not easy to accept failure and things that can't be controlled, but your child has to learn that impulse control is a necessary part of *anger* management.

Sometimes it is easy for parents to redirect their children into more appropriate behavior. Your child might just need some examples to try. When your child mutters to himself or says things under his breath, do not let this go unnoticed. Respond with, "No need to be disrespectful. Take a deep breath and think about what you want to say and how you want to say it."

> Children need self calming skills. This allows them to reflect on the reasons for their anger and to modify their reactions in the future.

Self-calming skills are essential in helping your *angry* child cool off. Such skills allow him to reflect on the reasons for his *anger* and to modify his reactions. When your child has a set of anger-reducing skills it is easier for him to get along with others and to know what to do in an adverse situation.

COUNT, BLOW, COUNT, BLOW

I was working with a four-year-old on how he plays in the playground and that sometimes his actions scare other kids. He was not a mean child but he did not know how to 'ask' for what he needed or wanted. I watched him play for several days and then had this conversation with him.

"Carl, when you want a sand toy, you need to use your words."

"But I do talk!"

"Yes, I saw that but when you pull your arm back, the other kids think you might hit them."

"I'm mad, if I don't get the bucket I want."

"If you can't use your words, you are going to have to cool off before you can play. When you want something you don't have, I want you to stop, put your hands deep down in the sand, and count to ten, blowing out each time after you count a number. Then think of what you want to say and say it."

We practice this a few times. Several days later I observed Carl just sitting with his hands deep in the sand pit. No other children are even around him.

"Carl, are you okay?"

"Ms. Julia, I need help."

"What do you need, Carl?"

"I want to cool off and use my words but I did as you said and now I can't play."

"Other kids won't play with you?"

"No, they want me to play but I can't ever finish cooling off. Go get Max," he asks me.

"Why?'

"I need Max," says Carl with urgency in his voice.

"But Max is not even playing near the sandpit. Why do you need Max?"

"Watch, one," he says as he pushes out his little lips and blows the same motion of putting out a birthday candle.

"Two, (blow), three, (blow), four (blow), five (blow), six (blow), seven (blow)," he looks up to me with big eyes. "I can only go on when Max is here because he know what comes next. Max is the best counter in the class."

I helped Carl count and blow on to the number ten and suggested that we change his plans and only cool off to seven because we would want him to do something he can do on his own without Max. When you work with your child, be prepared to alter or change plans as needed.

When children are angry, it's hard for them to understand their feelings. It's even harder to understand the feelings of others, but it's important for them to recognize that everyone else has feelings. When your child has empathy for others, he tends to be less aggressive and better liked by peers. You need to help your child be aware of the effect his negative behavior has on others, and you need to encourage him to accept help in managing his *anger*.

Recognize the target of your anger

It is hard to understand what fuels the fire of angry children. For many it is that they feel un-liked by others. They feel unworthy of having friends and unable to do anything right. I always have an *angry* child make a list of personal strengths. If he is unable to write, he will think of the strengths and I will scribe down what he says. We then identify the characteristics he would like to change or improve about himself. It is important to let him work on what he wants to change and not an adult's perception of what he should change. When they are able to develop personal strengths and achieve even small successes, they naturally feel better about themselves, and their *anger* gradually dissipates. It is important that children recognize the target of their *anger* and accept things they cannot change. For example, when there is a divorce in a family, children often are *angry*. Children need to be able to express this *anger* but also accept they can't change this outcome.

What things change?

Your child's facial expression will change as his emotions change. His body language will change. His posture will change and the tone of his voice will change. All of these changes let you know how your child is feeling. Some children communicate early signs of stressful feelings in subtle ways, such as frowning or sighing. If you notice your child starting to get upset, tell him what you notice and gently ask questions, "I see you are feeling upset. Please use your words to tell me what's wrong." Listening and letting your child know that you understand his feelings, teaches him that his emotions matter.

Listening and letting your child know you understand his feelings teaches him that his emotions matter. Some children communicate in subtle ways so tell them what you notice and ask them questions about what they are feeling.

When you feel your own face and body change due to emotions, it is important to be aware of it. This can be a 'teachable moment'. Explain to your child, and be honest. These comments will show your child much more than a command of cleaning up. "When I see this mess, my stomach gets a knot in it; I feel my face starting to get hot. I feel like I want to yell at this mess! Clean up! Can you understand what I am feeling?"

Depression is an alarming topic

The feelings of *anger* or depression should not be treated lightly. We recognize that the depressed person is not only *sad*; there are mixed feelings of pessimism and *hopelessness* and possibly *anger* as well. Davitz (1969), in *The Language of Emotion,* asked college kids to describe the ways they feel when they are depressed. He collected many descriptions of depression and this led to his conclusion that depression is a complex internal state having many elements. There are physical symptoms (tiredness, sleepiness), negative feelings about oneself (feeling vulnerable), impulse to action (wanting to withdraw), and physiological changes (no appetite). Any one of these is only a partial image of the complex state of depression. Not every child will have all of these feelings, but any one person might report several of these elements.

Depression in young children is a difficult topic for most parents to conceive or to accept. Children under stress, who experience loss, or who have attentional, learning, conduct or anxiety disorders are at a higher risk for depression. Depression also tends to run in families. The behavior of depressed children and teenagers may differ from the behavior of depressed adults. Child and adolescent psychiatrists advise parents to be aware of signs of depression in their youngsters.

A child who used to play often with friends may now spend most of the time alone and without interests. Things that were once fun now bring little *joy* to the depressed child. Children and adolescents who cause trouble at home or at school may also be suffering from depression. Because the youngster may not always seem sad, parents and teachers may not realize that troublesome behavior is a sign of depression. When asked directly, these children can sometimes state they are *unhappy* or *sad*.

Many children suffering from undiagnosed depression have been labeled as being shy, distant, lazy, stubborn, or disobedient. Depression affects the child's thoughts, feelings, behavior, and body. If they are old enough to talk, they may refer to themselves as stupid and ugly, disliked, unloved and incapable of being *loved*, *worthless*, or even hopeless. They may be preoccupied with themes of death and dying. Major depression in children and adolescents is serious; it is more than 'the blues'.

What do your actions teach your children?

Copying or imitating is a powerful form of learning. Babies and toddlers imitate adults. Even newborn babies can imitate. As children get older, their memory improves and this helps them learn even more from other people's action. Be careful what you do and say around babies and toddlers. By one year of age, babies can remember and imitate behavior they've seen four weeks ago according to ParentingCounts.com. When your child hears you say something or sees you do something that you wish you had not done, tell your child you made a mistake. Everyone makes mistakes. Explain what you wish you had said or done instead. If the bad example came from TV, Internet, in movies, or someone else, explain what you don't like about what happened. I call these 'teachable moments'. Help your child understand what is important to your family even if others might behave in a different way. Children need us to explain the difference between acceptable and unacceptable behavior.

Your Child is a Copy Cat

Children pay attention to the behavior of other children. They imitate what other children do. Younger children look up to older children. They often imitate the behavior of older children. Only choose TV shows and video games you would feel comfortable having your child copy.

Show me what to do

Children expect grownups to give them signals about what is okay and what is not okay. The younger the child, the greater their need to have clear examples of a wide variety of emotions and expressions. Parents can help children understand emotions by making sure their facial expressions match their verbal expressions and tone of voice.

Children expect grownups to give them signals about what is okay and what is not okay. The younger the child, the greater is his need to have clear examples of emotions and expressions.

By the time children are twelve-months-old, babies have learned to look at adult faces to make sense of unfamiliar things. A child will look at their parents and wait to see a smile or a nod before touching a new toy or new food. Your baby adapts more easily to new people, objects, and situations when you show positive emotions. One-year-olds are less likely to play with a new toy, if their mother reacts negatively to it, and are more likely to play with the toy if their mother seems positive about it. Babies, as young as 10-months-old, use information they see from other people's expressions to make their decisions on what is going on, according to the Talaris Institute. When your face says one thing but your voice or actions show a different feeling, your children will be confused.

The importance of building emotion stories

Working on these emotion stories, all children can develop a strong sense of personal narrative or their own voice. To foster this, I think two characteristics are fundamental: confidence and joyousness in telling the stories. A child should feel his story successfully communicates his specific meaning and emotion. You want it to convey his personal memories, ideas and feelings. If your child feels both happy and confident, he will be more likely to construct and communicate his emotions. The richer his vocabulary is in emotions, the more competent and powerful he will be in reflecting on his behavior and how his actions and interactions are intertwined.

Dilemmas and debates on moral development

Knowing your emotions can tie into knowing your 'values'. A mom stopped by my office and asked, "Should schools be responsible for teaching values? Why or why not? If not schools, then who? Parents can't do it alone. Is there such a thing as a set of 'common values' in a school where everyone is so mobile and you all have such varied backgrounds?"

After a very long discussion on the dilemmas and debates about moral development, we came to the conclusion that you should be looking for evidence of empathy and compassion in all students in the school. This starts with students knowing their own emotions. There are many different ways to look at moral development.

You are interested in all aspects of your child's development. In Jean Piaget's early writing, he focused specifically on the moral lives of children. He looked at the way children played games in order to learn more about children's beliefs about right and wrong (1932). Piaget concluded that schools should emphasize cooperative decision-making and problem solving, nurturing moral development by requiring students to work out common rules based on fairness. I still believe this is the best way to interact with children. In order to be successful, your child needs to have the emotion vocabulary and understanding when relating to his peers.

Moral Development Perspective

Framework	Theorists	Questions	Salient Elements of Response
Emotional Perspective	Hoffman, Zahn-Waxler, Eisenberg, Arsenio, and Tisak	How do you feel about the situation and what is your understanding of how others feel about the situation?	Looking for evidence of feelings (sympathy/empathy/compassion) and the lack of anti-social emotions (feeling happy that someone is sad).
Reasoning Perspective	Kohlberg, Piaget, Turiel, Smentana, Killen, Helwig, Waintrb, and Nucci	What are you thinking about in making your decision?	Looking for elements of domain distinctions among morality (harm, welfare, and rights), convention and personal domains: high character involves effective coordination among these domains within the boundaries of likely developmental considerations.
Caring	Noddings	In what ways are you taking into account your relationship with others in making your decision?	Looking for evidence of focusing on other person's perspective and doing the necessary work to see the other person's perspective (walk in their shoes).
Community of Practice Perspective	Etzioni, Bellah, Dunn, Tappan, and Miller	What do you think would be expected by your community (e.g. classroom) of you to do?	Looking for evidence that the child sees the community as providing the means to have good character; measuring both how the child perceives the community and the quality of the community in the classroom.
Competence Perspective	Freud, Bandura, Kuczunski, Grusec,	To what degree do other people's expectations affect your decision and how well do you feel you will be able to meet those expectations?	Looking for evidence that their actions are not dependent on the expectations of others because of sufficient self-efficacy.

What have you learned?

Complete the following learning table

Think

What things cause your child to get angry?

Talk

What moral development issues will you discuss with others?

Apply

What three actions will you apply and turn into a habit?

1.

2.

3.

Chapter Nine

Conclusion - when in doubt connect

One of the easiest ways to connect with a young child is to get them involved in a 'forced-choice' game. You simply ask your child to indicate which of two paired words is more descriptive of him or her: for example, is he or she more quarrelsome or shy? Take two equally undesirable traits or emotions; it is interesting to see if your child feels he is 'this emotion' or 'that emotion'. Is he bossy or naughty? Then choose two equally desirable emotions to see how your child sees himself. Is he kind or caring? It is great to build your child's understanding of emotions by asking them "do you think I am 'this' or 'that'?"

Young children begin the process of learning how to hide some of their emotional expressions, and many adults are adept at this. Some people are rewarded for having a 'poker face'. Adults are also capable of voluntarily creating any expression they wish regardless of how they may feel at the moment. You smile when you are sad. I've seen people appear friendly even when they are angry.

Attachment and expat children

In an expat child's life, grandparents, aunts, uncles, and cousins usually live thousands of miles away. You might only see each other for a family reunion or seasonal vacation. These important people have little influence on our children's lives as our children mature. Without a large array of healthy adult connection, the focus becomes exclusively on parents or guardians who are raising them. Some guardians are not known as the 'legal guardians' we are familiar with but as a local nanny who has been in your family for a while. It can be debilitating when these staff members change due to another move for your family.

For grandparents

Most relationships with grandchildren flourish because they get constant care and attention from their grandparents. There are many opportunities for expat grandparents to maintain and strengthen this special relationship. Technology is great for Skype, IM, face book, texting and blogging to each other. Webcams let you see what they are playing, doing, or experiences they are going through. Grandparents can read bedtime stories by video, share in birthday celebrations, and even see how tall their grandchildren have grown. Families can download photos, and videos, or write short or long updates about living overseas.

It can be a lot of fun to play Jeopardy or Wheel of Fortune online with a grandchild so don't rule out interactive Internet games as a way to create a bond. Parents *love* that grandparents can make custom crossword puzzles for the grandchildren to complete. But if Grandpa does the San Francisco Chronicle Sunday Crossword, parents can be sure their children's verbal skills will grow. If grandparents don't want to work with technology, all children *love* to get a special package from an overseas location with neat stamps.

In order to keep the grandparent connection, I have several families that use the '*anticipation* jar' as a focus to foster this involvement. To make sure your child knows when Grandma or Grandpa is going to see him 'next', you can count the days until they will be seeing each other again. You can take their favorite treat, such as M and

Ms, then count the exact number of days until Grandma or Grandpa will arrive and put the same number of candies in a jar. If you have more than one child, each child needs a counting jar. Your child gets to eat one piece of candy a day and when he sees the pile getting smaller, he will know that Grandma or Grandpa is 'coming'. This is a great visual aid that makes the time between visits easier to understand. Some families use pieces of dried fruit.

The ages of my children mean that they do not require a counting jar, but with Jackie off in college, I am tempted to try this. Then I realize that the excitement of seeing her is almost already too much to handle that perhaps adding sugar to the mix will just increase my state of excitement. I need a 'parent counting the days to see the child' instead of a child counting to see a parent or grandparent. That saying "They grow up before you know it" is indeed true in my household.

Anytime is a good time to start creating new family rituals. Traditions can get passed down from generation to generation. Expat children need this connection to their history.

This is a great time to start creating new family rituals. Something that kids can do with their grandparents to make the world seem a little smaller after a big move overseas is to focus on a point that you have in common, such as the moon. For example, tell your grandchild that the same moon that they see is the same moon that you see. If they are having a hard time in school, or have just had a bad day, they can send a special 'message' through 'moon mail'. The moon can deliver the message, and they know that when you look up and see the moon you will always automatically think of them and send your *love* back through 'moon mail'. Traditions like these are often the ones that get passed down to their kids and grandkids.

You might want to read Pat Burn's book, *Grandparents Rock* and visit the website www.grandparents.com

Risk factors for expat children

Risk factors are personal or environmental characteristics that predispose a person to a negative developmental outcome. Psychologist Mark Katz (1997) describes risk factors as those events, experiences, or conditions that increase the chance that a person will have problems. One of his main concerns is when your child does not bond to a school because of frequent moves. No matter how we look at it, your child's school is a social event for him.

There are also conditions known as protective factors, factors that buffer against, or mediate, the risk of developmental failure. Sometimes a child's personality, intelligence, and bonding to teachers and school serve as protective factors that help him have a much more successful outcome. One approach to the study of risk and protective factors comes from the work of the Search Institute (Seales and Leffort, 1999). Since 1980s, the Search Institute has been surveying sixth to twelfth graders in more than 600 communities across the U.S.A. Their quest was to identify those developmental assets or building blocks that all youth need to grow into healthy, caring, principled, and productive adults.

They show these building blocks to include:

- Positive emotional tone and relationships with peers and parents

- Satisfaction with life

- Academic achievement

- Responsible attitude toward sexual behaviors

- Positive adjustment during school transitions

Reflections on moving

Working in international schools, you always have key times when families move. There is a large turn over after the school year every summer and at Christmas time. But of course, not all international schools are on the American calendar so children arrive and leave throughout the school year. Understanding the cycle of transitions is a key need for parents of these young expat children. Older children need to understand the cycle themselves and how they adjust to things.

From *According to my Passport, I am going home*

Cecile M. Mines conducted a discussion of moving and reentry with Foreign Service children aged four to nine. She found them to be quite amazingly articulate about their feelings about moving. At the end of Mines' session, she put a block of wood, a piece of felt cloth, a pine cone, a piece of sandpaper, and a silk scarf on a table and had the children choose an object that felt like they had felt when they moved.

One girl chose sandpaper, "Because it was rough. My aunt took a lot of my stuff and we had to find new homes for my pets."

Another, choosing wood, said, "It was very, very, very hard to move because I had to leave a lot of my friends and my cat behind."

A nine-year-old chose the felt cloth because, "It was not hard like the wood or rough like sandpaper or gooey like the pine cone. It was smooth but a little harder than the scarf...a little warm and soft because my parents let me do lots of things and let my friends come over every day."

The seven-year-old boy said, "I would pick all of them.... Rough because I had to leave behind my friends, easy because the school is better here...hard to leave my cats behind but easy because no more sneezing."

I work a lot with transitions at international schools. When I ask the question, "What was your biggest transition?" children will think for just a few seconds and then quickly respond. It does not matter what their ages are. It happens with five-year-olds and with 18-year-olds. Children know how each and every transition has impacted their life and how it has made them feel. They do not label every transition, but they do know which one was the 'biggest'. Many transitions are given a 'best thing ever' rating. Children understand and want to talk about what their life has been being an expat child.

The ability to repair

> Interactions between parents and young children are full of disruptions, miscommunication, and misunderstandings. We need to connect so we can repair.

All parents make mistakes. The interactions between parents and their young children are full of disruptions, miscommunication, and misunderstandings. This is the reality of all of our lives. Researchers have found that perfectly in-tune moments happen less than one third of the time in typical mother-infant pairs (Tronick, 1989). What makes a relationship feel secure is the ability to 'repair'; your child can feel safe in the understanding that when mistakes or disagreements happen, you will pay attention to the cues they are sending, try to understand what they need, and come back again. There is always another chance to connect.

Make Repairs

No parent and child are perfectly in-tune. Learning that, being temporarily out of sync doesn't mean the end of the relationship. This is an important lesson for your child to understand before they get to an age where there are bound to be disagreements or times you can't be in sync.

What have you learned?

Complete the following learning table

Think

What is the easiest way to connect with your child?

Talk

What miscommunication or misunderstandings will you like to talk about and discuss with others?

1.

2.

3.

Apply

What will you do to connect with your family?

Love – Fifth Stage to a Strong Connection

When you walk through the living room and just smile at your child, resisting the impulse to ask if he's done all of his homework or walked the dog, you are giving him love. When a child does not feel this elemental basic love coming from his parents, he will look for it from peers.

Chapter Ten

Closing comments

Many individuals have helped me as I researched this book. The most important are the young people (from my schools) themselves who have been amazingly open and wonderfully articulate. I *love* working with families in international schools. These children are so worldly and wise. Ruth Hill Useem states. "They adapt. find niches, take risks. fall and pick themselves up again. Many indicated they feel at home everywhere and nowhere."

> ### Being Known – Sixth Stage to a Strong Connection
>
> From age six onward, if the attachment roots have gone deeply enough, we have a child who allows him or herself to venture out into Being Known.

Without my children. Jacqueline and Grant. I would never have begun the process of finding out about the effects of emotions on young people. and without my husband Kevin, none of us would have had a global lifestyle.

I am appreciative of John F. Kennedy University Clinical Psychology program that gave me a firm foundation in child. adolescent and family therapy. Their motto states "Transforming lives. Changing the world." This is very true in my situation with families around the world. I am grateful to Summertime Publishing for publishing this material for a growing generation of global young children and their parents.

Even though this book was written for young children, it is never too late to start collecting memories of your emotions. This is especially true for children who are global nomads. Due to the fast pace of your lives now, you seldom have time to close certain chapters. We get on a plane and within hours of departing one area we land in another area. We close one chapter of our lives. We start up a new chapter in our new life in a new location. Parents locate new homes, establish new routines, and hire new 'quasi family members'. Families start all over again. As we Skype, twitter, and blog ourselves around the world, we need to take time out to collect some emotional memories that are beneficial for the whole family.

For parents - a note from your child

Thank you for taking time to help me complete our emotion- memory stories.

"Now . . . we speak the same memories . . ."

Emotion quotes to ponder:

One of the best resources for emotion quotes can be found at
http://www.thefreedictionary.com/Emotions , these are some of my
favorite quotes.

- Emotions buzzed and throbbed ... like a pent-up bee —
  Elizabeth Bowen

- Emotions got cut off ... like a broken string of beads —
  Susan Fromberg Schaeffer

- Emotions ... swarm in my head like a hive of puzzled bees
  — Gertrude Atherton

- Emotion akin to a physical blow — Henrietta Weigel

- Feeling full of wonder and illusion — like a Columbus or a
  pilgrim seeing the continent of his dreams take shape in the
  dusk for the first time — Richard Ford

- Feelings bubbled in him like water from an underground
  spring — Paige Mitchell

- Feelings cross our flesh along nets of nerves, like a pattern
  of lightning flashes —Marguerite Yourcenar

- Feelings...jumbled together like raveled wool — Frank
  Swinnerton

- Felt as small and vulnerable as a calf on its first day of life
  — Linda West Eckhardt

- Felt like a lifeline thrown out to someone — Mike Feder

- Felt like an emotional invalid, like a balloon without the helium — T. Coraghessan Boyle

- Felt worry and joy flinging her about like a snowflake — Mary Hedin

- Half smiles, half tears, like rain in sun — John Greenleaf Whittier

- Love and emptiness in us are like the sea's ebb and flow — Kahlil Gibran

- Our feelings have edges, spines and prickles like cactus, or porcupines — Laurie Colwin

- (A feeling of) relief circles us like a spring breeze — Richard Ford

- Relieved [after things have been put right] … like they lifted a concrete block out of my belly — John Updike

- Stirred an emotion … like the birth of a butterfly within a cocoon — Adela Rogers St. Johns

- Too moved to even applaud … as if the air had been sucked out of the room — Samuel G. Freedman

- Truth and jealousy, like a team of plow horses, came crashing into the fragile barn of his illusions — Louis Auchincloss

- A vague uneasy stirring plagued her like some mental indigestion — Josephine Tey

- A warm feeling like cocoa on a cold night — Jean Stafford

- Wore his confidence like a tailored suit — Donald McCaig

Useful resources

Books – must reads if you are raising an expat

Altman, Irwin and Low, Setha, *Place Attachment*

Bell, Linda, *Hidden Immigrants: Legacies of Growing Up Abroad*

Bowers, Joyce, (Editor) *Raising Resilient MKs: Resources for Caregivers, Parents and Teachers*

Burns, Pat, *Grandparents Rock: The Grandparenting Guide for the Rock-n-Roll Generation*

Bryson, Debra R. and Hoge, Charise M., *A Portable Identity: A Woman's Guide to Maintaining a Sense of Self while Moving Overseas*

Davis, Gabriel, *The Moving Book*

Eidse, Faith and Sichel, Nina (ed), *Unrooted Childhoods*

Flournoy, Robert, *Just a Little Rain (Military Brats)*

Greenberg, Barbara R. and Powell-Lunder, Jennifer A., *Teenage as a Second Language: A Parent's Guide to Becoming Bilingual*

Halpern, Justin, *Sh*t My Dad Says*

Hess, Melissa and Linderman, Patricia, *The Expert Expatriate: Your Guide to Successful Relocation Abroad*

Hickman, Katie, *Daughters of Britannia: The Lives and Times of Diplomatic Wives*

Hughes, Kathryn, *The Accidental Diplomat: Dilemmas of the Trailing Spouse*

Knell, Marion, *Families on the move*

Kohls, Dr. L. Robert, *Survival Kit for Overseas Living: For Americans Planning to Live and Work Abroad*

Larson, Aaron, *Dads at a Distance: An Activities Handbook for Strengthening Long Distance Relationships*

Larson, Aaron, *Moms Over Miles: An Activities Handbook for Strengthening Long Distance Relationships*

Jehle Caitcheon, Ngaire, *Parenting Abroad*

Kalb, Roselind and Welch, Penelope, *Moving Your Family Overseas*

Marx, Elizabeth, *Breaking Through Culture Shock*

McCluskey, Karen Curnow, *Notes from a Traveling Childhood*

Pascoe, Robin, *Homeward Bound: A Spouse's Guide to Repatriation*

Pascoe, Robin, *A Moveable Marriage*

Pascoe, Robin, *Raising Global Nomads*

Pollock, David and Van Reken, Ruth, *The Third Culture Kid Experience: Growing up among Worlds*

Quick, Tina L., *The Global Nomad's Guide to University Transition*

Roman, Beverly, *Footsteps Around the World: Relocation Tips for Teens*

Roman, Beverly, *Home Away from Home: Turning Your International Relocation into a Lifetime Enhancement*

Romano, Dugan, *Intercultural Marriage: Promises and Pitfalls*

Shepard, Steven, *Managing Cross-Cultural Transitions: A Handbook for Corporations*

Smith, Carolyn D., *Strangers at Home: Essays on the Effects of Living Overseas and Coming "Home" to a Strange Land*

Steinberg, Gregg, *Flying Lessons: 122 Strategies to Equip Your Child to Soar into Life with Competence and Confidence*

Storti, Craig, *Figuring Foreigners Out*

Tokuhama-Espinosa, Tracey, *Raising Multilingual children*

Walters, Dr. Doris, *Missionary Children: Caught Between Cultures*

Westphal, Chris, *A Family Year Abroad: How to Live Outside the Borders*

Julia's Top 30 Books for Five-year-olds

1. Alexander, Claire, *Lucy and the Bully*
2. Blohm, Judith, M., *Where in the World Are You Going?*
3. Brown, Marc, *D.W.'s Guide to Preschool*
4. Cain, Janan, *The Way I Feel*
5. Carlson, Nancy, *Look Out Kindergarten Here I Come*
6. Child, Lauren, *I Am Too Absolutely Small for School*
7. Couric, Katie, *The Brand New Kid*
8. Cummings, Carol, *Finding Feelings*
9. Curtis, Jamie Lee, *It's Hard to be Five!*
10. Cuyler, Margery and Yoshikawa, Sachiko, *Kindness is Cooler*
11. Deal, Russell, *The Wrong Stone*
12. Hickman, Martha Whitmore, *I'm Moving*
13. Joosse, Barbara and Lavalle, Barbara, *Mama, Do You Love Me?*
14. Henkes, Kevin, *Wemberely Worried*
15. Lovell, Patty, *Stand Tall Molly Lou Melon*
16. Lucas, David, *Halibut Jackson*
17. Ludwig, Trudy, *Sorry*
18. McCormick, Wendy, *Daddy, Will You Miss Me?*
19. Meiners, Cheri, *Understand and Care*
20. Myers, Bernice, *It Happens to Everyone*
21. O'Neill, Alexis, *The Recess Queen*
22. Pak, Soyung, *Sumi's First Day of School Ever*
23. Penn, Audrey, *The Kissing Hand*
24. Rockwell, Anne, *Welcome to Kindergarten*
25. Rylant, Cynthia, *The Relatives Came*
26. Verdick, Elizabeth and Heinlen, Marieka, *Words Are Not for Hurting*
27. Ward, Heather Patricia, *I Promise I'll Find You*

28. Wells, Rosemary, *Mama Don't Go*
29. Wickens, Roth, *My first Day of School*
30. Wolff, Ashley, *Miss Bindergarten Gets Ready for Kindergarten*

Excellent Websites

http://www.amongworlds.blogspot.com

http://www.anniefox.com/cruel.php

http://www.brucelipton.com/

http://cafepress.com/tck

http://www.ceop.police.uk/

http://www.denizenmag.com/?p=54

http://ecis.ccsct.com/page.cfm?p=1

http://www.expatmumsblog.com/

http://www.grandparents.com

http://www.happierkidsnow.com

http://www.happyfornoreason.com/Home.asp

http://www.hayhouseradio.com/hosts.php?author_id=184

http://www.iss.edu/

http://www.mkplanet.com

http://www.overseasbrats.com

http://www.psi-solutions.org/experts/kalman/

http://www.TCkid.com

http://www.transition-dynamics.com

http://www.whatsyourbodytellingyou.com/

Bibliography

Barr, R. & Hayne, H, (1999). Developmental changes in imitation from television during infancy. *Child Development,* 70 (5), 1067-1081.

Blanchard, D.C. & Blanchard, Robert. *Defensive Behaviors, In: George Fink, (Editor-in-Chief) Encyclopedia of stress, Second Edition, volume 1, pp. 722-726. Oxford: Academic Press.*

Bruner, J. (1986). *Actual minds, possible worlds.* Cambridge, MA: Harvard University
Press.

Camras, L. A. & Allison, K. (1985). Children's understanding of emotional facial expressions and verbal labels. *Journal of Nonverbal Behavior,* 9, 84-94.

Davitz, J. (1969). *The language of emotion.* New York: Academic Press.

Denham, S. A. & Burton, R. (1996). A social-emotional intervention for at-risk 4-year-olds. *Journal of School Psychology,* 34(3), 225-245.

DeVries, R. & Zan, B. (1994). *Moral Children: Constructing a Constructivist Atmosphere in Early Education.* New York: Teachers College Press.

Dooley, Cate and Fedele, Nikki (1999). *Mothers and Sons: Raising Relational Boys,* JBMTI papers.

Domitrovich, C. E., Cortes, R. & Greenberg, M. T. (2002, June). *Preschool PATHS: Promoting social and emotional competence in young children.* Paper presented at the 6th National Head Start Research Conference, Washington, DC.

Eakin, Kay Branaman. *According to my passport I'm coming home.* Family Liaison Office, June 1, 1998

Ekman, P. (1993). Facial expression and emotion. *American Psychologist,* 48, 384-392.

Ekman, P. & Friesen, W. V. (1986). *A new pan-cultural facial expression of emotion. Motivation and Emotion,* 10, 159-168.

Fujiki, M., Spackman, M. P., Brinton, B., Illig, T. (2008). *Ability of children with language impairment to understand emotion conveyed by prosody in a narrative passage. Department of Communication Disorders,* 130 TLRB, Brigham Young University, Provo UT.

Galati, D., Miceli, R. & Sini, B. (2000). Judging and coding facial expressions of emotions in congenitally blind children. *International Journal of Behavioral Development,* 24, 226-278.

Galati, Dario, Sini, Barbara, Tinti, Carla & Te, Silvia. The lexicon of emotion in the neo-Latin languages. *Social Science Information* June 2008 vol. 47 no. 2 205-220

Gibson, E. J. & Walk, R. D. (1960). The "visual cliff". *Scientific American,* 202, 67-71.

Goleman, Daniel (1998) *Working with emotional intelligence.* New York: Bantam Books.

Gopnik, A., Meltzoff, A. N. & Kuhl, P. K. (1999). *The Scientist is the crib: Minds, brains and how children learn.* New York: William Morrow.

Gottman, J. Talaris Institute (2004). *What am I feeling?* Seattle, WA: Parenting Press

Greenberg, M. T. & Kusché, C. A. (1998). Preventive interventions for school-age deaf children: The PATHS curriculum. *Journal of Deaf Studies and Deaf Education,* 3(1), 49-63.

Heider, K. G. (1991). *Landscapes of emotion: Mapping three cultures of emotion in Indonesia.* New York: Cambridge University Press.

Izard, C. E. (1971). *The face of emotion.* New York: Appleton-Century-Crofts.

Izard, C. E. (1977). *Human emotions.* New York, London: Plenum.

Izard, C. E., Fantauzzo, C. A., Castle, J. M., Hayes, O. M., Rayias, M. F. & Putnam, P.H. (1995). The ontogeny and significance of infant's facial expressionism in the first 9 months of life. *Development Psychology,* 31 (6), 997-1013.

Kemper, T. D. (1987). How many emotions are there? Wedding the social and the autonomic components. *American Journal of Sociology,* 93, 263-271.

Landis, C. & Hunt, W. A. (1939). *The startle pattern.* New York: Farrar, Straus & Giroux.

Lewis, M. & Brooks-Gunn, J. (1979). *Social cognition and the acquisition of self.* New York: Plenum Press.

Lewis, Sullivan, Stranger and Weiss, Deception in 3-year-olds. Developmental Psychology 25 (1989), pp. 439-443.

Lyons, Michael J. (2000). *Viewpoint dependent facial expression recognition Japanese Noh Masks and the human face.* Institute for Research in Cognitive Science, University of Pennsylvania.

Moore, B. & Beland, K. (1992). *Evaluation of Second Step, preschool-kindergarten: A violence prevention curriculum kit. Summary report.* Seattle, WA: Committee for Children.

National Scientific Council on the Developing Child (2004). Children's emotional development is built into the architecture of their brain. http://www.developing child.net/pubs/wp/Children's Emotional Development Architecture Brains.pdfTips.

Neufeld, Gordon and Mate, Gabor, Hold on to Your Kids: Why Parents Need to Matter More than Peers, Ballantine Books, 2006.

Plutchik, R. (1962). *The Emotions: Facts, theories and a new model.* New York: Random House.

Plutchik, R. (1989). Measuring emotions and their derivatives. In R. Plutchik and H. Kellerman (1989) (Eds.) *The Measurement of Emotions* (Vol. 4, pp.1-36). New York: Academic Press.

Pollock, D. (1987). *Reaching Out to Third Culture Kids.* Trans World Radio 8, No. 5,
November/December, 1987.

Repacholi, B. M. & Gopnik, A. (1997). Early Reasoning about desires: Evidence from 14-18 months olds. *Developmental Psychology,* 33(1), 12-21.

Russell, J. A. (1983). Two pan-cultural dimensions of emotion words. *Journal of Personality and Social Psychology,* 45, 1281-1288.

Schweder, R. A. & Hoidt, J. (2002). The cultural psychology of the emotions: Ancient and new. In M. Lewis and J.M. Haviland-Jones (Eds.), *Handbook of Emotions* (pp. 397-414).

Shaver, P. R. & Hazan, C. (1988). A biased overview of the study of love. *Journal of Social and Personal Relationships,* 5, 473-501.

Sorce, J. F., Emde, R. N., Camps, J. & Klinnert, M. D. (1985). Maternal emotional signaling: Its effect on the visual cliff behavior of 1-year-olds. *Development Psychology,* 21 (1), 195-200.

Storm & Storm (1987). A taxonomic study of the vocabulary of emotions. *Journal of Personality and Social Psychology,* 53, 805-816.

Warren, S. L., Emde, R. N. & Sroufe, L. A. (2000). Internal representations: Predicting anxiety from children's play narratives. *Journal of American Academy of Child and Adolescent Psychiatry,* 39, 100-107.

Webster-Stratton, C. & Hammond, M. (1997). Treating children with early-onset conduct problems: A comparison of child and parent training interventions. *Journal of Consulting and Clinical Psychology,* 65(1), 93-109.

Wehrle, T., Kaiser, S., Schmidt, S., Scherer, K. R., (2000). Studying the dynamics of emotional expression using synthesized facial muscle movements. *Journal of Personality and Social Psychology,* 78, 105-119.

White, G. M. (2000). Representing emotional meaning: Category, metaphor, schema, discourse. In M. Lewis and J. M. Haviland-Jones (Eds.), *Handbook of Emotions.* New York: Guilford Press.

CPSIA information can be obtained
at www.ICGtesting.com
Printed in the USA
LVOW12s0102260417

532192LV00002B/19/P